HOW TO BE A GOOD PARENT

"Create your own way"

Professor Larry Jensen

ARPress
ILLUMINATING IDEAS,
EMPOWERING VOICES

ARPress
45 Dan Road Suite 5
Canton MA 02021
Hotline: 1(888) 821-0229
Fax: 1(508) 545-7580

Ordering Information:
Quantity sales. Special discounts are available on quantity purchases by corporations, associations, and others. For details, contact the publisher at the address above.

Printed in the United States of America.

| ISBN-13: | Softcover | 979-8-89330-056-7 |
| | eBook | 979-8-89330-057-4 |

Library of Congress Control Number: 2024901175

TABLE OF CONTENTS

PREFACE

This book asks you to create your own way to be a good parent because no two parents can or should be alike and no two children are the same. Good parenting then becomes a creative process; it is not achieved by adopting wholesale the rules, techniqes and styles of others. Fortunately, the best parenting will come easily and naturally for you and this book reveals how to make this happen.

Beginning in 1956 and continuing to the end of the century I studied psychology, conducted and published scores of reseach based articles in reputable academic journals, and published a university level texbook on parenting. I also wrote a self directed teaching manual for my parenting class. Upon these writings rests the foundation, documentation or references for this book that I put before you at this time.

I retired my Professorship during the first year of the 21st century and this lead me to reflect on my parenting of 3 step children, 1 adopted child, 3 natural born children along with observing how they parented 33 grandchildren over the following 22 years. My observations and reflections confirmed what I had published about parenting and added some more insights. These new insights, based on lived experience, were incorporated into this book along with revising much of the content to make it more pratical and easy to apply.

An important part of this book are the self tests or learning experiences designed to help you examine and develop your way to be a good parent. In essence it asks you to create you own theory of parenting designed uniquely for you as you relate to each unique child. It is not written to be read passively but activly as you are presented questions and asked to thoughtfully answer them to achieve your own special way to be a good parent.

INTRODUCTION:

Parenting Is for You

After reading the introduction, you should be able to do the following:

1. Discuss why the most important predictor of being a successful parent is how much you enjoy your children.

2. Describe ways to increase your ability to enjoy children.

3. Define areas of self-development that will result from being a parent.

Principle 1

It is better to enjoy what you do than to do what you enjoy.

Idea No. 1: The best predictor of successful parents is parental enjoyment.

The above conclusion came from a research after extensively studying 379 mothers of kindergartners in the Boston area. First, mothers were evaluated on more than one hundred child-rearing practices. Personal records and background information on each mother and child were meticulously recorded. Twenty-five years later, when the children were thirty-one years old, another team of researchers located and evaluated seventy-eight of the children. They judged maturation on the basis of independence, self-reliance, How a mother feels about her child is the key to her success. How can parents do right by their children? If they are interested in promoting moral and social maturity in later life, the answer is simple--they should love them, enjoy them, want them around. They should not use their power to maintain a home that is designed for the self-expression and pleasure of adults. They should not regard their children as disturbances to be controlled at all costs. . . It was the easygoing, loving parents whose children turned out to be the most mature. Is that a remarkable finding? Isn't it just common sense? The trouble with common sense is that it is so uncommon. [1] and genuine concern for others. They were careful to obtain information about friendships, work experiences, illnesses, memberships in organizations, and whether they had been in trouble with the law. Surprisingly, researchers did not find that specific child- rearing practices were good predictors of personal growth and maturation. [2]

Idea No. 2: The key to parental success is in how the parent feels about the child.

To illustrate this "uncommon" common sense, we will read firsthand reports from students about family life. Personal experiences are important not only as illustrations of concepts, but also because they provide realistic insights. Staying close to firsthand and up-to-date accounts of the parenting process enables us to keep in touch with the common sense that is not so common. In addition to firsthand reports from students about family life, we can draw common sense from the statements and opinions taken from parents participating in parenting workshops. In general, these sources of information concur with the conclusions of the Harvard research. [3]

One of the more popular points of view among child development specialists is that of perceiving a child as analogous to a seed. Basically, a seed holds the blueprints—DNA, if you will—for what he will eventually become. The seed analogy emphasizes the genetic and biological characteristics that will "blossom" or develop with maturation. This perception allows for great individual differences— differences which are inherent and evident from birth or early childhood. Much research supports this concept of inborn individual differences. [4]

Now you are asked to complete a short exercise. Each principle presented in this book is followed by one or more of these learning exercises. They are not difficult to answer. In fact, you may think they are too easy; that may be true but the challenge is not whether you can answer them correctly, but whether you learn something about yourself when answering these questions. Also, the important point may not be whether you believe something but how strongly you feel about it.

LEARNING EXPERIENCE 1.1

Self-Test on Enjoying Children

To help you understand some of the beliefs associated with enjoying children, complete the following self-evaluation. Circle the answer that most nearly describes your opinion about each belief. Then, compare your answers with a partner and discuss any differences in opinion. **(KEY: SA=Strongly Agree; A=Agree; U=Uncertain; D=Disagree; SD=Strongly Disagree)**

1. It is more important to work with children than to win power struggles.

    SA   A   U   D   SD

2. Mistakes in parenting are to be expected.

    SA   A   U   D   SD

3. Happiness comes through giving rather than receiving.

    SA   A   U   D   SD

4. Having a helping partner is preferable to parenting alone.

    SA   A   U   D   SD

5. Children are opportunities rather than responsibilities.

    SA   A   U   D   SD

6. Parents can't make their children happy but they can provide an environment to engender happiness.

    SA   A   U   D   SD

7. Associating with child-oriented friends is preferable to my associating with singles groups.

    SA   A   U   D   SD

8. Children are basically good; they just need guidance from parents and other responsible adults.

    SA   A   U   D   SD

9. Having a sense of humor is important in raising children.

SA   A   U   D   SD

10. You need to plan your schedule around your children rather than your children around your schedule.

SA   A   U   D   SD

11. It is important that the parent not be manipulated by the child.

SA   A   U   D   SD

SCORE	**TOTAL NO.**
Strongly Agree	_____
Agree	_____
Uncertain	_____
Disagree	_____
Strongly Disagree	_____

The higher the agreement level, the more likely you are to enjoy being a parent.

LEARNING EXPERIENCE 1.2

Self-Planning Form for Enjoying Children

Using the self-evaluation results of Learning Experience 1.1 and the information in the research quoted in Idea No. 1, complete the following form in consultation with either your marriage partner or with someone else in order to enlarge your perspective about these issues.

1. Am I a person who can enjoy raising children?

2. What are some things I can do or ways I can feel that will help me enjoy children more?

3. What are some things I can stop doing or feeling that will help me enjoy children more?

4. How will enjoyment of children increase my effectiveness as a parent (teacher or leader)?

Principle 2

Finding what you want for your family.

Idea No. 1: Families can live together without power struggles or harsh discipline.

My parents always treated me with a great deal of respect, as I did them. I was never rebellious. I always felt close to them and knew they loved me very much. Very little harsh discipline was administered, mainly because it was not necessary. I never really had a desire to see how far I could push my parents and don't remember ever being spanked. A disappointed tone in my parents' voices was all I needed to make me feel remorse.

A student made this statement in one of our parenting classes. Many family members—parents and children—seek this type of relationship but it is elusive. Even when it seems to have been captured, often it still slips away.

Idea No. 2: "Harmonious Parenting" is a viable option.

One psychologist found eight couples living in the Berkeley, California area who was able to sustain this type of family atmosphere, which she called "Harmonious Parenting". She wrote the following.

[Harmonious parents] focused upon achieving a quality of harmony in the home, and upon developing principles for resolving differences and for right living...Harmonious parents were equalitarian in that they recognized differences based upon knowledge and personality, and tried to create an environment in which all family members could operate from the same vantage point, one in which the recognized differences in power did not put the child at a disadvantage. They lived parallel to the mainstream rather than in opposition to it. In their hierarchy of values honesty, harmony, justice, and rationality in human relations took precedence over power, achievement, control and order, although they also saw the practical importance of the latter values. [5]

Learning Experience 2.1 is designed to help you identify areas in your family experience which you want to improve or keep the same. What you discover about your family experience will prove useful in subsequent principles as you apply the information gleaned to meet your goals. Parenting is such a big job and so complicated that it is hard to monitor everything. It is especially hard to know where to begin making improvements while considering the feelings of your spouse and children.

LEARNING EXPERIENCE 2.1

Self-Test on Harmonious Parenting

Now, to help you explore your own feelings after having completed these experiences and finished the readings, conclude by reading the following statements and circling the answer that best describes how you feel about each statement. **(ANSWER KEY: SA=Strongly Agree; A=Agree; U=Uncertain; D=Disagree; SD=Strongly Disagree)**

1. Parents can guide children effectively without using harsh discipline.

    SA   A   U   D   SD

2. Families can live together without power struggles or harsh discipline.

    SA   A   U   D   SD

3. Harmonious parenting focuses on resolving differences without harshness or power struggles.

    SA   A   U   D   SD

4. Harmonious parenting focuses on achieving harmony in the home through values, honesty, justice, rationality, and respect for individual differences.

    SA   A   U   D   SD

5. Mere expression of disappointment can change children's behavior in an atmosphere of respect.

    SA   A   U   D   SD

6. Children who feel loved and close to their parents do not need as much parental discipline to guide their actions.

    SA   A   U   D   SD

Principle 3

Parenting is for the parent too.

My first baby awakened the lioness instinct that causes a mother to protect the baby, fending off jackals of all sorts. As I have dealt with doctors, businessmen, teachers, and neighbors, my courage has increased. But the crowning event occurred when I had three boys ages one, two, and four, and I was six months pregnant. My husband was at a youth conference and I was alone. In the middle of the night, I heard a noise downstairs. My first thought was, "My boys are in the other room!" I grabbed my husband's baseball bat and went downstairs with fire in my eyes. Either there was nothing there or I scared off whoever or whatever it was. Suddenly I realized what I had done—had faced the dark. I was never afraid of the dark again.

Idea No. 1: Parenting changes parents.

One of the most provocative books written about parents and children is *Child Affects on Adults*. [6] The authors pointed out that children influence their parents. Belsky, Steinberg, and Draper [7] also present a theory proposing that parents change as a result of the parenting experience. We propose that parents experience personal growth as a result of raising children. This happens because of small growth- promoting events for both the mother and father. Consider the following statement: How does this happen? There are several reasons, which we will explore.

Idea No. 2: Reproduction and child-care help parents become better people.

Pregnancy: The first effect a child has on the mother is in altering her physiology during pregnancy. Hormonal changes in turn affect the size and function of the mother's body. She experiences new emotional states. For nine months the mother lives with the inescapable knowledge that she is responsible for supporting two lives.

[8] If the parents of the prospective child continue to communicate closely during the pregnancy, then they both will realize that they are not alone and that their lives are already intertwined with the life of a yet unknown person.

Childbirth: In the past, childbirth was considered a life-threatening experience for women and, in fact, was one of the leading recorded causes of death among women. Although safer now, the birthing process still involves much trauma and pain for the mother. [9] The father's presence during the birthing experience may well impress upon him the possibility of losing the mother and increase his appreciation for her sacrifice.

Caring for the Newborn: The newborn is helpless and requires complete and constant care from the mother. The infant's survival depends upon this care. The mother is responsible for feeding, cleaning, dressing, warming, comforting, and protecting the child. As with pregnancy, the mother continues to be accountable for the well-being of the child. When the father is present in the family, he will recognize the necessity of the mother's involvement with the child. Selfishness on the part of either parent can conflict with the responsibilities of the mother and father.

Child Care: Children require almost as much constant care as infants. During childhood, a child must be trained, disciplined, and educated in all aspects of life that are important to the culture of the parents. A responsible parent will devote a considerable amount of time to these tasks. The devotion of parents may also awaken feelings of adoration within themselves. Assuming this role may even change how adults view themselves and the world. Ainsworth's attachment theory [10] clearly demonstrates the attachment that parents and children somehow undergo. Other research [11] supports this belief in high levels of care and attachment during these early years.

Bonding: The process of bonding has been noted by psychologists from both the biological and social perspectives. ([12]) When humans bond they seem to view their lives, well-being, happiness, pain, and sorrow as inseparable. Bonding creates feelings of closeness and empathy that defy definition.

Bonding has been substantiated to occur between mothers and infants, and now it is believed that fathers and their infants also bond. [13] Generally, research indicates that stronger bonding and more secure attachment occur when parents spend more time with their infants. Other research shows that bonding occurs between mothers and fathers as they build their lives together. When two form a bond, it tends to create a feeling of concern for the other person that overrides concern for the self. Thus, one could reasonably expect a change in the personal characteristics of parents as the result of bonding. By bonding and relating to a child, a parent can scarcely escape the increased levels of selfless concern for another life as well as increased awareness of life and the opportunities that the bonding experience can bring about with regard to mental, social, and emotional growth.

Time and Resources: A mother typically devotes time and effort to both her spouse and her child. In an agricultural setting, children were an economic asset. In an urban city setting, the value of children to parents is less well understood. Nevertheless, parents in the city still devote a great deal of time and energy to raising children and as a result of these efforts, most parents develop in character. [14]

Shift in Personal Responsibility: The life events described above require a change in behavior on the part of the parents. This change occurs as parents learn to act for the welfare of others, which requires time and sacrifice. [15] This aspect alone is sufficient to influence the emotional, personal, and social growth of parents. The actions, however, are not as influential as the change in a parent's frame of mind following the birth and rearing of children. The process of raising children causes one to view life differently. This may be more dramatic in the case of the mother, but the father is impacted as well. The most significant shift is from the self-oriented perspective typical of childhood and adolescence to a perspective that emphasizes the welfare of others. By placing the welfare of another person on the same or a higher level than one's own, a new aspect of human growth can be realized.

Idea No. 3: Parents say that they see growth in self and spouse.

We asked students in introductory human development classes to give surveys to parents belonging to the following ethnic groups: American-Caucasian; Austrian-Caucasian; Chinese; Filipino; Hawaiian; Japanese; Korean; other Asians; and Samoan. The students mailed or personally administered six survey booklets to three sets of parents who had successfully raised at least one seventeen-year-old. The survey asked the parents to rate the amount of change they believed had occurred in their spouses during the parenting years. The results of the survey are presented in Table 3.1. Please spend a few minutes studying Table 3.1.

TABLE 3.1

Percentage of parents who said there was a great increase in the following areas of personal development in their spouses since parenting.

Gread Increast in:	MEN	WOMAN
Ability to Love	42%	53%
Character	31%	39%
Patience	44%	50%
Less Selfish	35%	41%
Organization	21%	36%
Personal Strength	32%	41%
Personal Worth	33%	36%
Sense of Humor	37%	26%
Knowledge of People	40%	41%
Social Skills	33%	27%
Religious Experience	35%	37%

Approximately 97 men and 133 women had complete data for these questions, so there are slight variations.

Average number of children:	2
Ages of the eldest children ranged from:	3 to 60 years
Percent describing themselves as middle class:	85%

Represented a wide variety of religious denominations Ethnic Group representation: American-Caucasian, 88; Austrian- Caucasian, 11; Chinese, 8; Filipinos, 22; Hawaiian, 32; Japanese, 20; Korean, 21; Other Asian (mostly Chinese), 11; Samoan, 16;

Idea No. 4: Fathers as well as mothers change because of parenting.

After studying Table 3.1 you will probably conclude that across cultures, parents report a great deal of personal growth in their spouses.

A surprising finding was the high level of change reported for men. The change took place in all of the cultures studied so we feel confident in concluding that there is a significant amount of personal development among fathers during the parenting years.

It is our opinion that no other experience—work, school, religion, or even one's own childhood—is a more powerful influence on adult behavior and personality than the experience of raising children. The intensity of the experience is greater because of the high level of emotional involvement parents have with their children over the course of several decades.

Idea No. 5: The major change in parents is a shift from the self-centeredness of childhood and adolescence to the unselfishness of parental responsibility.

We also believe that the parenting experience changes men and women in a positive direction because it requires the parent to act unselfishly. It requires them to break from their childhood and adolescent self- centered views and focus on the care of others. For this reason, we believe that the experience is significant and deserves coverage in the field of psychology as a legitimate factor in the explanation of adult behavior. You now have the opportunity to evaluate the amount of change you expect to experience during the parenting years by completing Learning Experience 3.1.

LEARNING EXPERIENCE 3.1

Welcoming Growth in Self and Spouse

It always helps to have a little something special for yourself. This is true for parenting as well. But what you receive for yourself may not be what you expected. As you know, parents give and give. Children take your time, your money, your spouse's attention, and seem to give nothing in return. What you receive is not readily apparent—it is delayed and covert—but by completing the following evaluation you can discover what it is that you will receive for your years of sacrifice and devotion. Then you can decide for yourself if it is worth the effort.

For each of the characteristics below, please indicate the amount of change that you believe will occur for your husband/wife during the years you raise your children. Then, repeat the evaluation for yourself.

Change for Spouse	Great Increase	Average Increase	No Change	Decrease
Ability to Love	1	2	3	4
Character	1	2	3	4
Patience	1	2	3	4
Less Selfish	1	2	3	4
Organization	1	2	3	4
Personal Strength	1	2	3	4
Sense of Personal Worth	1	2	3	4
Sense of Humor	1	2	3	4
Knowledge of People	1	2	3	4
Social Skills	1	2	3	4
Religious Experience	1	2	3	4
Other	1	2	3	4

Change for self

Ability to Love	1	2	3	4
Character	1	2	3	4
Patience	1	2	3	4
Less Selfish	1	2	3	4
Organization	1	2	3	4
Personal Strength	1	2	3	4
Sense of Personal Worth	1	2	3	4
Sense of Humor	1	2	3	4
Knowledge of People	1	2	3	4
Social Skills	1	2	3	4
Religious Experience	1	2	3	4
Other	1	2	3	4

Now take a moment to ponder what you said when responding to the above evaluation. The gift you will receive which we were discussing is the gift of personal growth. It's not money, vacations, or even a nicer house but something far more enduring--personal characteristics that will bring you joy in living.

SUMMARY

Instructions: Mark *a* if the statement is true and *b* if it is false. Submit to instructor.

1. The best predictor of successful parents is parents who are organized and have definite expectations.

2. There are certain beliefs that can help you enjoy children more.

3. There are things that I can do that will help me enjoy children more.

4. Families will always have power struggles.

5. Harmonious parenting focuses on achieving harmony in the home through values and respect.

6. Being a parent helps individuals become better people.

7. Childbirth, caring for the newborn, and child care are all activities which are demanding and detract from a woman's personal development.

8. Mothers, but not Fathers, say that they see growth in themselves as a result of being a parent.

9. The key to parental express is how the parent feels about the child.

10. Bonding occurs between parents and children but not between parents and parents.

LESSON ONE

Making Parenting Positive

After you have successfully completed this lesson, you should be able to do the following:

1. Explain why the role of parent is the most important role in life.

2. Compare the costs and rewards of having children.

3. Define ways to handle parenting stress.

Principle 4

You do best that which is important to you.

Idea No. 1: The importance of supplying physical necessities is often underestimated.

In 1991, I had the opportunity of spending the last six months in the country of Papua New Guinea. It is a mystical country, relatively untouched by the outside world. Most people live in extreme poverty. A person is fortunate to own one change of clothes, and shoes are rarely seen.

I was humbled when I once encountered a pregnant woman hauling seventy pounds of water balanced on her head and shoulders. It was a duty she performed daily as the water was used by a large family. My companion and I helped her carry the water home where we were introduced to the other ten members of this family which was housed in a one-room tin shed with a dirt floor. Three of the children were suffering from malaria-the family had eaten nothing but coconuts and taro roots for three days. The father would do anything to get some food for his family.

We offered this man work which he gladly accepted. At the end of the day he was paid with some rice and tins of fish. We accompanied him to his home and felt great joy as we watched his family feast upon the fruits of his labor.

We are fortunate that we rarely have to concern ourselves with physical needs or safety. We seem much inclined to take for granted our comforts and security. Since we don't have to worry about those needs, we often become self-centered and focus on our personal social needs and achievements. The family mentioned above and many others in New Guinea awakened in me the importance of meeting one's physical needs and especially the importance of doing so as a parent.

My father worked very hard and was a very busy man. Each day after working his eight-hour shift he would change his clothes and head to the farm. He then farmed until it was too dark to see. Because of irregular water turns, my dad spent a good portion of his nights up irrigating. According to him, there just weren't enough hours in the day.

Despite his busy schedule and the many projects he had to do, my dad always made time for his children, sometimes in very creative ways. Three of my sisters ran track in high school.

Most of their meets started in the early afternoon, making it difficult for Dad to attend them. He would decide which meets were most important for him to attend and schedule them in his planner. I couldn't begin to count the number of times my dad showed up at my sisters' track meets with a sticker on his shirt which read, "Be nice to me, I gave blood today."

When urgent projects at the farm made this difficult, Dad would turn family home evening into "family farm evening," or "family hoe evening." For holidays, Dad always planned something with the family like hiking, camping, or fishing--whatever we wanted to do.

My dad gave his children time when we most needed it. His family has always been his first priority.

Idea No. 2: Many parents work hard and make sacrifices for their children.

Another example that illustrates how important the role of a parent is comes from the child of a man in the armed services:

The role of raising children is added to the role of providing for the family for almost all fathers. In addition, there are many other important, meaningful, and desirable things to do in life. It is hard to choose between them because so many are both important and enjoyable. However, all parents must prioritize their activities and give their limited time and money to some rather than others. We asked parents to rate the importance of being either a mother or a father and also to tell us which are the most significant roles in life. We found that for all cultures, the role of mother was rated number one and the role of father was rated number two (See Table 4.1 on the next page). Compared to other activities, the activity of raising good children was also rated number one as shown in Table 4.2.

It is interesting to consider by what criteria one could judge parenting as unimportant or without challenge. If one were to do a task analysis, as occupational counselors do, one would be hard-pressed to find any profession that requires more intellectual, physical, and maturity skills than does being a successful parent. A parent has almost total responsibility for raising the most complex organism on the planet. Not only does the parent procreate the most complex organism, but the parent is totally responsible for all aspects of this organism's development including physical health, emotional security, and intellectual development. The successful parent must also understand the elements involved in the child's maturing process as well as the world surrounding the child. No profession or career is more challenging or significant.

Completing Learning Experience 4.1 will help you discover your feelings about the importance of parenting. After careful consideration you will probably find that the prestigious professions actually have less permanent impact on human life than does parenting. Changing diapers and listening to children's chatter or separating fighting children are not particularly glamorous activities, but if you compare the realities of what appear to be the most glamorous professions, you will find that all that glitters is not gold. These prestigious positions have a downside to them which sometimes could make dealing with diapers, jabbering children, and refereeing siblings seem highly desirable by comparison. Now please complete Learning Experience 4.1 according to the instructions given.

TABLE 4.1

Average ranking given to nine roles by mothers and fathers across cultures

Rank	Roles	Average Ranking Men (n=82)	Average Ranking Women (n=99)	Average Ranking Men/Women (n=181)
1	Mother	1.65	1.67	1.66
2	Father	2.27	2.43	2.36
3	Elementary Teacher	3.50	3.25	3.36
4	Physician	4.79	4.91	4.86
5	Scientist	5.06	5.09	5.08
6	U.S Senator	5.13	5.22	5.18
7	Film Celebrity	5.35	5.25	5.30
8	Researcher	5.33	5.33	5.66
9	Poet	5.83	5.81	5.91

A low average means that it is positive being closer to the rank of number one.

TABLE 4.2

Average ranking given by mothers and fathers to the ten activities across cultures

Rank	Roles	Men (n=81)	Women (n=100)	Average Men/Women (n=181)
1	Raising good children	2.28	2.30	2.29
2	Worshiping supreme being	4.29	3.36	3.33
3	Financial Security	4.23	4.64	4.46
4	Being competent in profession	4.70	5.22	4.98
5	Learning	5.40	4.95	5.15
6	Serving others	5.14	5.25	5.20
7	Enjoying life	5.38	5.30	5.34
8	Being the best in someone area of life	5.81	5.63	5.71
9	Travelling	5.91	5.76	5.83
10	Enjoying art	5.99	5.81	5.89

A low average means that it is positive and closer to the rank of number one.

LEARNING EXPERIENCE 4.1

Importance of Parenting Scale

Outstanding carpenters, athletes, teachers, seamstresses, farmers, or musicians have something in common—they like what they do. They believe their work is important and they enjoy it. You probably won't enjoy parenting if you don't think that parenting is important. To help you evaluate how important parenting is to you, rank the following statements according to their importance. Please rank the following activities from 1 to 14. Begin by putting a "1" in front of the statement which you believe is most important then continue through number 14.

_____Accomplishing things and meeting personal challenges

_____Achieving respect and admiration from others

_____Developing personal abilities and talents

_____Performing public service

_____Raising good children

_____Obtaining financial security

_____Experiencing as much as possible and traveling

_____Learning as much as possible

_____Enjoying life as much as possible

_____Serving others

_____Enjoying and participating in the arts

_____Worshiping a supreme being

_____Becoming the best in some area of life

_____Being competent in occupation or profession

Which of the following professions gives a person the greatest opportunity to have a significant impact on society? Please rank these from 1 to 9 beginning with number 1 as the greatest opportunity.

_____Mother

_____Father

_____Scientist

_____Elementary school teacher

_____Physician

_____Film celebrity

_____National government leader

_____Renowned poet

_____Researcher

Principle 5

Children can be rewarding.

Idea No. 1: Sometimes "hard times" are actually "good times."

I grew up in the little town of Marikana, Manila, Philippines. It is an island near the center of Manila. My father was a wealthy businessman. He put himself through school and learned early the importance of hard work. My mother was a manager of our clothing and shoe store. I was twelve years old when I realized how much we had compared to the poverty-stricken families that lived near us. We had four maids, six drivers, six trucks, and four cars. Even though we had all these things to enjoy, my parents taught me and my brothers and sisters how to be responsible by working together around the house. My parents set up chore assignments. We had our own dishes, and if we didn't wash them, we had to eat on a dirty plate. We scrubbed floors, walls, did gardening, cleaned cars, shopped, cooked, washed clothes by hand, etc.

I was able to work closely with my brothers and sisters, and I can truly say that I loved those moments. We had so much respect for each other. Many consequences did evolve, both good and bad, from those experiences. My parents used positive and negative punishment in dealing with our mistakes. I never felt that they were punishing us-just the behavior-because they never stopped giving us hugs, kisses, and warm emotion. I really felt that I belonged to this family. This type of experience helped me to be responsible, mature, and self-reliant.

My parents often told me that material things are temporary and if our situation should change, our ability to work together would save us from adversity.

The adversity that my parents had mentioned came when I was four years old. The recession came and the government took my father's business. It was a sad time for everyone. We worked hard even to obtain our food. We ate one meal a day, mostly from what we had grown in our back yard, but the sense of responsibility remained, and it pulled us together

Idea No. 2: The rewards and costs of raising children are perceptions in your mind and can be changed.

Even if you were to conclude that parenting is important, you might find that you still view children as interfering with your personal happiness. One researcher in the Los Angeles area studied how women viewed the rewards and costs of being a parent and working. [15] In her study she found there were definite costs and rewards to being a parent. To enjoy being a parent, the rewards should outweigh the costs. Consider, however, that these rewards and costs are really cognitive perceptions and can be changed. These rewards and costs are perceptions, *not* facts.

To help you assess the relative strength of your perceived rewards and costs of parenting, the following scale has been adapted from this researcher. By completing the scale you should be able to find out if the costs loom larger than the rewards for you. Please turn to Learning Experience 5.1 to help you assess the relative strength of your perceived rewards and costs of parenting.

LEARNING EXPERIENCE 5.1

Part One: Rewards of Children Scale

Here are some statements sometimes given as *good things* or *advantages* to being a parent. For each statement, please mark the number that most correctly indicates how important this reward is for you. If it is very important, rate with number 5; if it is not important at all rate with number 1. **(SA= Strongly Agree - 5; A=Agree - 4; U=Uncertain - 3; D=Disagree - 2; SD=Strongly Disagree - 1)**

	SD	D	U	A	SA

1. I can contribute to society by raising a good person.

       1   2   3   4   5

2. I enjoy doing things with children.

       1   2   3   4   5

3. Having children could help me grow and develop as a person.

       1   2   3   4   5

4. I can observe the growth and changes that occur in children.

       1   2   3   4   5

5. I enjoy taking care of children.

       1   2   3   4   5

6. I could feel a sense of pride in my children's accomplishments.

       1   2   3   4   5

7. I like the idea of having a family.

       1   2   3   4   5

8. Children can be a comfort to me when I grow older.

       1   2   3   4   5

9. Children strengthen the bond between husband and wife.

       1   2   3   4   5

10. Children help to carry on the family name and traditions.

         1   2   3   4   5

11. I would like the challenge of being a parent.

         1   2   3   4   5

12. Children are an expression of love between husband and wife.

         1   2   3   4   5

13. I could aid in the development and learning of another human being.

         1   2   3   4   5

14. I like the special feeling of love that develops between a parent and child.

         1   2   3   4   5

15. Children would keep me feeling young.

         1   2   3   4   5

16. Having children gives a sense of fulfillment.

         1   2   3   4   5

17. I feel that a part of me would live on after my death.

         1   2   3   4   5

18. Children would provide me companionship.

         1   2   3   4   5

Now complete Learning Experience 5.2 - Costs of Children

LEARNING EXPERIENCE 5.2

Part Two: Costs of Children Scale

Here are statements sometimes given as *bad things* or *disadvantages* to being a parent. For each item, circle the number that indicates how important it is to you. If it is very important, rate with a number 5 for **STRONGLY AGREE. (SD=Strongly Disagree; D=Disagree; U=Uncertain; A=Agree; SA=Strongly Agree)**

	SD	D	U	A	SA

1. I'm worried about the kind of world my children will grow up in.

    1   2   3   4   5

2. I would worry about my children's health and well-being.

    1   2   3   4   5

3. Children involve high financial costs.

    1   2   3   4   5

4. Children involve discipline problems.

    1   2   3   4   5

5. Having children contributes to the population problem.

    1   2   3   4   5

6. Children can sometimes be disagreeable and irritating.

    1   2   3   4   5

7. Children would interfere with my employment.

    1   2   3   4   5

8. I would feel guilty about spending time away from my children.

    1   2   3   4   5

9. There would be less time to do other things I'd like to do.

    1   2   3   4   5

10. It's hard to find good people to take care of your children.

        1   2   3   4   5

11. I have doubts that I would do a good job as a parent.

        1   2   3   4   5

12. Children create a lot of extra work.

        1   2   3   4   5

13. Children limit freedom and privacy.

        1   2   3   4   5

14. Children create problems and stress between spouses.

        1   2   3   4   5

15. I don't have the patience for raising children.

        1   2   3   4   5

16. Children cause noise, mess, and annoyance.

        1   2   3   4   5

17. Children don't always turn out the way parents want.

        1   2   3   4   5

18. Raising children involves a great deal of responsibility.

        1   2   3   4   5

To determine if the rewards of parenting outweigh the costs for you:

A. Add up the points from columns "A" and "SA" in Learning Experience 5.1 and enter the number here:

TOTAL "A"

B. Add up the points from columns "A" and "SA" in Learning Experience 5.2 and enter the number here:

TOTAL "B"

If you would like to enjoy children even more, there are some choices that can help you. We learn and are influenced by our environment to like and dislike certain activities. Choices we make on a daily basis can put us in circumstances that will either hinder or enhance our enjoyment of children.

The cliché that "You can lead a horse to water, but you can't make him drink" is true as far as it goes. But, you can influence him to drink by influencing his thirst! The horse tied in the barn all day or who has spent the afternoon jogging along a hot, dusty trail is going to be thirsty when led to water. Since our friends, our lifestyles, and our perceptions determine if we can and will enjoy children, we might say that associating with children is akin to influencing our thirst. We will have far more positive experiences with children than we will have negative ones and those positive experiences can create a thirst within us for more of the same, IF we allow it to happen.

Unless parents enjoy children, all the sophisticated child-rearing techniques in the world cannot result in successful parenting. On the other hand, as research indicates, parents who genuinely enjoy children are those whose children have the best chance of becoming competent, capable, and mature adults.

Hopefully, completing Learning Experience 5.3 will give you some insights about attitudes and choices that will help you enjoy children more.

LEARNING EXPERIENCE 5.3

CHOICES TO HELP YOU ENJOY CHILDREN MORE

The statements and attitudes that will influence enjoying parenting

1. Mistakes in parenting are a natural part of parenting.

   "We learn from our mistakes."

2. Humor and flexibility help in guiding children.

3. Learning communication and behavior management skills will help reach children.

"There is a way to reach every child."

4. Parenting is a special way of life.

   "Turn around and he's three, turn around and he's four, turn around and he is a young man going out of the door."

5, Your mate is your first line of assistance.

   "It's more fun when we enjoy the children together."

6. Reserve specific time for children.

   "Let's put this on my calendar."

CHOICES THAT DON'T HELP

1. I must be a perfect parent.
   "What if I do something wrong?"

2. Being serious and rigid will instill responsibility.

3. There's no way for an adult to reach children.
   "I don't work well with children."

4. I'll always be taking care of children.
   "Life is passing me by."

5. The children are your responsibility.
   "Look what your kids have done."

6. Children's needs must be worked into my schedule.
   "I have to finish this project and then I can talk to you."

Principle 6

How to handle stress

I felt overwhelmed. There didn't seem to be time to finish anything during the day. Then dinner was usually late, and when we finally sat down to eat with the 7:30 news, it felt like the whole evening was gone. There was no free time.

These are the words of a young woman who left her full-time job just before her first child was born. She looked forward to the complacent life of cooking gourmet meals, putting up preserves, baking bread, gardening, writing in her journal, and spending relaxing days with the baby.

Idea No. 1: Most parents face some stress in the parenting role.

This is one of four women described in the December 1982 *Parents* magazine who had to learn to deal with stress. Fathers, too, must learn to cope with stress. If you haven't noticed by personal observation, common sense tells you that parenting stress is inevitable. Therefore, learning to cope with this stress is a high priority in parenting.

Flight, denial, willpower, and drugs all are unsuccessful ways in which parents respond to stress. The best-selling drugs in the country are stress medications but drug use is not the answer. Stress is a major medical problem and researchers have discovered successful ways to cope. They have also discovered some basic contributors to increased stress such as lack of planning, lack of flexibility, role overload, and unrealistic expectations.

Dr. Hans Selye, [19] author of *Stress without Distress* and a pioneer in distress research, believes that you cannot avoid stress because to eliminate it would destroy life itself since stress, when properly utilized, is healthful both physically and psychologically. Dr. Selye's solution to dealing appropriately with stress is to become aware of the sources of your stress and then learn to cope with them.

To help you identify the origin of your stresses, read the items listed in the following questionnaire and check those items which apply to you.

Idea No. 2: Both men and women need help coping with parenting stress.

These sources of stress in the parenting context apply both to men and women. However, women generally feel parenting stress more acutely because they most often assume the primary child-rearing role. The methods for coping with stress, however, apply equally to men and women. Since you have already identified your personal sources of stress, the next step is to learn to cope with them.

Idea No. 3: The four steps to successfully handling stress

Step 1 - Attack the Sources of Stress.

Since lack of planning is followed by too much to do with not enough time available, the first step in coping is to develop daily and weekly plans of action. It is important in these plans of action to list what needs to be accomplished on a priority basis. Write down what needs to be done and then review this list to prioritize what MUST be accomplished.

Be flexible. It might be valuable for you to memorize the following quotation to recite when your plans are disrupted and require adjustment: ***"God, grant me the strength to change what I can, the serenity to accept what I cannot change, and the wisdom to know the difference." Decide for yourself that fighting the "waves" in life is not worth the emotional distress produced.***

Choose those issues which are worthy of stress by realistically evaluating incidents that could produce stress. Sometimes a child's "rough-housing" in a particular room or receiving low grades in school does cause stress but are these incidents creating sufficient damage to warrant your anguish? In many cases stress occurs as a result of mentally creating it rather than its actual existence. So, evaluate whether the stress you feel is actual or self-inflicted.

Step 2 - Find Help.

There are resources to help a parent who is experiencing stress. The first source of assistance should be the spouse. In an issue of *Parents* magazine the author listed several ways to motivate men to help their wives. 16 Both husband and wife can and should lean on each other for emotional and physical support. Additionally, older children can often successfully assume major responsibilities within the home which not only helps the parent but contributes to the child's self-development.

Extended family is another resource that may be called upon when needed. Many a young mother gains a greater appreciation for relatives (especially her mother or father) when she has their support in caring for the young child.

Parents should not be averse to the hiring of household help or babysitters when family members are unavailable or live beyond the range of convenient travel. Many young mothers have discovered that the benefit derived from this expense is well worth the price.

Friendships with other parents can often provide a resource for sharing experiences, babysitting, shopping, and other activities. These are primarily physical ways in which friends can help each other with their child rearing. Emotional support can also be gained from friends who are willing to listen empathetically and offer suggestions.

Finally, community resources sponsored by government, church, and school organizations to help parents rear children, should not be overlooked. Investigate the resources available in your community. You will probably be surprised at the number and variety of services and helps available.

Step 3 - Physical Health

While stress is often caused by environmental, social, and emotional pressures, many stress reactions result from poor physical conditioning.

You should evaluate your daily schedule to determine if it allows for adequate sleep and if your eating habits are within established guidelines for good nutrition. Routine physical examinations can identify physical and medical problems that contribute to stress and need treatment. With the nationwide emphasis on physical fitness, the benefits of regular exercise are now being better understood. Sufficient and appropriate physical exercise can result in better diet and nutrition, improved emotional stability, and greater physical strength and stamina. Honestly evaluating one's physical condition and taking steps to improve where needed are very important steps in coping with stress.

Step 4 - Activity and Rest

The final step to be considered in dealing with stress recognizes the value of fun and relaxation. Industry has successfully utilized these two principles as a way of assisting employees in dealing with stress. In the home, recreational and physical activities as well as rest times can, and should, be scheduled on a regular basis. Frequently, young mothers find that the only time they have to rest is during their child's nap time. These nap times should be used to the mother's advantage either in obtaining more sleep or for personal rest and relaxation. So-called "power naps" of even 15 minutes can give a parent a second wind in dealing with their daily challenges.

Prior to marriage the basic lifestyle and relaxation of young adults was probably dating. Most young couples find that it is important to continue dating after marriage, at least on a weekly basis. In addition, getting out with other couples for fun and relaxation is a good way to not only strengthen the relationship but to reduce some of the stresses inherent to that relationship.

Idea No. 4: Humor helps relieve stress in parenting.

Robert Eliot, a University of Nebraska cardiologist, gave two rules for coping with stress: "(1) Don't sweat the small stuff, and (2) It's all small stuff." 18 I frequently tell my children that happy people are happier.

This ridiculous saying should only be heard from a father but it is one way to "lighten up" when a mole hill is becoming a mountain. Some people do become easily upset by the small but inevitable incidents of daily life. People who become easily upset are certainly more unhappy. No one seeks out stress unnecessarily or enjoys the panicky feeling of being overwhelmed but these feelings are largely a matter of choice. There are only two ways with which to respond to these ongoing complications of life without creating unnecessary stress: first, change what can be changed and second, accept what cannot.

Parenting is a challenging role where stresses are inevitable because of children's demands, problems, and pressures. Also, the stresses in families are stronger because of the emotions involved and our concern for those we love. To be successful we must accept the reality that a certain amount of stress will always be present and then develop a plan to cope with it.

To help you evaluate your personal tendencies where stress is concerned, and to reinforce the coping strategies presented in this principle, please complete Learning Experience 6.1.

LEARNING EXPERIENCE 6.1

Personal Stress Tendencies and Practices

Circle the term which most nearly describes your feelings about each statement. (**SA=Strongly Agree; A=Agree; NS=Not Sure; D=Disagree; SD=Strongly Disagree**)

1. I often feel stress when I fail to plan ahead.

    SA   A   NS   D   SD

2. When I set very high expectations and am not able to meet them, I feel stressed.

    SA   A   NS   D   SD

3. I have lower levels of stress when I try not to anticipate problems and focus on only those problems that actually occur.

    SA   A   NS   D   SD

4. I often feel stressed when I "spread myself thin" by trying to do too many things.

    SA   A   NS   D   SD

5. When I stay up late and don't get enough sleep, I am less able to cope with stress.

    SA   A   NS   D   SD

6. When I don't eat properly or exercise and have poor health, the stresses of daily living/parenting affect me more.

    SA   A   NS   D   SD

7. When I plan ahead I resist changing plans or adapting to changes by others.

    SA   A   NS   D   SD

8. When I feel stressed, I often find myself ignoring demands placed on me by others.

    SA   A   NS   D   SD

9. I try to be flexible and adaptable in meeting the demands of daily living/parenting.

SA   A   NS   D   SD

10. I try to anticipate many future problems and often cannot sleep because of thinking or worrying about them.

SA   A   NS   D   SD

LEARNING EXPERIENCE 6.2

Stress Coping Planning Form

Having completed the stress evaluation in Learning Experience 6.1, you are now prepared to select methods for coping with stress. Circle any item, "a" through "f" that would help resolve the issue presented in numbers 1 through 4.

1. Cope with stress by:
   a.   developing daily and weekly plans
   b.   increasing flexibility by learning to accept what you can't change
   c.   facing problems directly
   d.   identifying times to sleep such as when a baby sleeps, etc.
   e.   realistically evaluating stressful events
   f.   resisting the urge to take on too much

2. Find help through:
   a.   spouse
   b.   older children
   c.   relatives
   d.   hired home help or babysitter
   e.   friends
   f.   church and community resources

3. My physical condition needs:
   a.   sleep scheduling
   b.   program for good nutrition
   c.   physical checkup and medical care
   d.   regular exercise

4. Activities to evaluate:
   a. physical activities
   b. recreation
   c. rest times
   d. dates with spouse
   e. getting out with children and other couples
   f. getting out without children

SUMMARY

Instructions: Mark *a* if the statement is true and *b* if it is false. Submit to Instructor.

1. One would be hard pressed to find a profession that requires more physical, intellectual and maturity skills than does being a successful parent.

2. Next to a physician and scientist, mothers and fathers receive the next highest ranking across cultures.

3. Providing financial security and serving others are the two most important roles for men and women as reported in the research.

4. The rewards and costs of children are perceptions in your mind, but cannot be changed.

5. It is not possible to compare the rewards to the costs of raising children.

6. There are two things that help you enjoy children more.

7. One way to help you to enjoy children more is to identify attitudes and choices that you would like to strengthen and also find those that you would like to discontinue.

8. The four steps to successfully handling stress are: 1) attack the source; 2) find help; 3) physical health; and 4) humor.

9. Failing to plan ahead, setting very high expectations, and spreading myself thin are three out of the ten activities that cause personal stress.

10. It is possible to learn to cope with stress by analyzing the sources of stress and finding sources of help, developing your physical health, and increasing certain activities.

LESSON TWO

Home: A Good Place for Fathers

After you have successfully completed this lesson, you should be able to do the following:

1. Identify reasons for having children.
2. Determine the roles and activities for both mothers and fathers in the parenting process.
3. Discuss the role of and service required of the "head of the household."

Principle 7

Finding your reasons for having children

One of the reasons my parents had children was because it was expected of them--because of social pressure. They were expected to have children within a year after their marriage or else other people (family and friends) would think something was wrong with their marriage or that they had some physical problems.

Researchers Hoffman and Hoffman[22] reviewed a number of studies and developed nine basic reasons for having children:

1. Adult social status and identity

2. Expansion of self, tie to a larger entity, immortality

3. Morality, religion, altruism, good of the group, sexuality norms

4. Primary group ties, affiliation

5. Stimulation, novelty, fun

6. Creativity, accomplishment, competence

7. Power, influence, effectiveness

8. Social comparison, competition

9. Economic utility

Let us discuss these further. You will like some of these reasons and dislike others. That is to be expected. The important task is to discover *your* own reasons. Hopefully, you will be able to do this by the end of the lesson and also see how your reasons influence your parenting.

Idea No. 1: Having children for social status and identity.

The first reason for having children, adult social status and identity, is largely a production of social expectations. Society defines a mature and growing marriage as one including children. This pressure to become parents is encountered from different sources: from statements by parents and parents-in-law like "When are you going to make us grandparents?"; from neighbors who ask, "Do you have any children?"; from peers; and from a pervasive sense of adhering to society's expectations.

Idea No. 2: Having children for a sense of immortality.

For some adults, having children assures a sense of immortality—a means of passing oneself on into unforeseen generations. One student provided an example of how children might be seen as an expansion of the self—an opportunity for one to live on:

One of the things I have seen parents enjoy about their children is experiencing parts of their own lives, which they feel they missed out on, through the lives of their children. My husband's family is quite wealthy and I have noticed this happen in his family. His father and mother both started as small-town farm children; they worked themselves up to where they are today. Because they couldn't have many of the things they wanted when they were young, they give these things to their children. One of the youngest children has a horse collection that was his mother's idea. . . . My husband. . . was also given a new car and put through college. In some ways I feel the parents enjoy it all more than the kids do.

Idea No. 3: Having children for religious and moral reasons.

The third reason for having children as cited by Hoffman and Hoffman is that many adults choose to become parents due to religious and moral beliefs. Bringing children into the world is a divine part of the overall plan of life. To have children signifies faith, obedience, virtue, and respect for authority. This view is seen in our Judeo-Christian heritage, "Lo, children are an heritage of the Lord; and the fruit of the womb is his reward" 20 (Psalms 127:3). Consider the view of one student who said:

I think one reason people have children. . . is because it is a command of God. We are told to multiply and replenish the earth. . .[they] feel guilty if they don't have kids.

Individuals not condoning any particular formal church may consider child-rearing as altruistic, unselfish, and a means of sustaining their culture.

Idea No. 4: Having children as primary group ties and for affiliation.

I have a friend who says she has kids so she can do things with them when they get older. She's always saying that she can hardly wait until her children get old enough to go shopping, go on camping trips, etc.

This is a big part of why my husband and I want a family also. We love being with people; having a family will give us a ready-made group to do things with.

One reason for having children involves affiliation and group ties. My mother was an only child. She always wished she had brothers and sisters to play with and to go to school with. She had twelve children.

Children are esteemed as sources of satisfaction and affiliation. The family is seen as a refuge against loneliness and isolation; having children helps create a refuge. For women, children might provide desired warmth and affection.

Idea No. 5: Having children for stimulation, novelty, and fun.

One student stated:
The reason my friend had children was because she was bored. Her husband worked long hours, and she didn't have enough thing to occupy her time. She wanted children for stimulation and for something to do.

Many men and women feel that children are fun and a source of happiness. The joys of child-rearing seem to outweigh the trials and difficulties. Parents sometimes find it easier to establish a family routine and to forget outside troubles when children are in the family. A recollection of their own experience as children, such as remembering vacations and family outings, creates a desire to replicate some of those feelings with children of their own.

Idea No. 6: Having children for a sense of accomplishment.

Another value and reason for having children is perhaps the most obvious to many people. A child's achievements are sources of a parent's pride. These may even be used by parents to compare with other children's accomplishments as a measure in evaluating their own parenting success. The role of parenting can also contribute meaningfully to feelings of competence. Consider the following examples:

Idea No. 7: Having children for power, influence, and effectiveness.

My uncle and his family are good examples of having children as a source of competence. The more children they had, the more important they felt. They had four children before my parents even had one, and it was always mentioned in their conversations--"all his wonderful kids." He ended up with ten, and they were very proud of it.

My father came from a small town where the entire population was employed by one factory. His father and grandfather were also employed there. It seemed to him that working at the factory was all that was waiting for him also. So, he moved to a town where there were lots of opportunities for different jobs. He started to expect his children to really make something out of their lives. Whenever we went back to visit my relatives in that small town, my father would always show off my brothers and me. My father shows off his accomplishments and reminds his brothers and sisters that they and their children are still working in the factory.

Historically, numerous children, especially in underdeveloped countries have ensured the survival of the family unit. In an agrarian society, many hands make lighter work and in small communities a large family, especially with adult children can have a greater influence on the governmental and community affairs of their town.

Idea No. 8: Having children for social comparison and competition.

While many people may mention this reason in a favorable way, it seems to lack many positive outcomes. Nevertheless, you should consider whether you are motivated by this reason.

Idea No. 9: Having children for economic utility.

While the standing joke about a woman preparing to deliver toward the end of December usually involves the possibility of a "new tax deduction," there are other economic principles involved in having children. One of those is the security created by having children involved in a family business, which has been one of the firmest foundations upon which the economic balance of a country may be maintained.

Different cultures sometimes have unique reasons for having children; you will have to identify your own reasons to really understand the motives you might have for becoming a parent. It is also important to know your partner's views on having children in order to have a harmonious relationship.

To further understand your motives for parenting, continue with Learning Exercise 7.3.

LEARNING EXPERIENCE 7.3

How Do My Reasons for Having Children Influence My Parenting Behaviors?

Indicate how much you agree with the following statements by circling the appropriate response: (**SA=Strongly Agree; A=Agree; NS=Not Sure; D=Disagree; SD=Strongly Disagree**)

1. Having children brings adult status but also requires adult levels of unselfish concern for the welfare of those dependent upon me.

SA   A   NS   D   SD

2. Children provide a way for parents to influence the future and contribute to society, so it is important to help children make a positive contribution to society.

SA   A   NS   D   SD

3. Part of my desire to have children is based on my religious principles and sense of what is good and right, and I want to help my children adopt these altruistic values.

SA   A   NS   D   SD

4. Having children provides family associations, so I want to make our family a happy place to be.

SA   A   NS   D   SD

5. Children give us purpose in life, so I want to focus my efforts on helping my children become the best they can be.

SA   A   NS   D   SD

6. Children can give a sense of pride to parents, so I want to raise my children in a way that I can be proud of them.

SA   A   NS   D   SD

Principle 8

The importance of the father

Idea No. 1: Parents support each other and give each other encouragement.

During winter semester I was going to school and working part time taking care of three little kids. It sure opened my eyes; I had every responsibility a parent would have but no spouse to help. Let me tell you that task is nearly impossible. Try cooking dinner, holding and rocking a fussing baby, and cleaning the mud off the two other kids all at the same time. I would come home completely exhausted from trying to be aware and on top of everything that went on that day. If you think that left any time for me, you are wrong. I began to really understand the importance of having someone else there to take things off my hands and give me a chance to breathe.

Not only does a spouse give you that helping hand when you are about to break, but they also give you the male encouragement to keep you strong when you normally couldn't do it by yourself. Whenever I feel just a little inadequate or under-qualified, just a simple look or smile from my husband will give me the strength or self-esteem to face the next challenge. Sure, I probably could make it on my own if I had to, but I would much rather go through this life with someone else beside me helping me along the way.

The above story gives an example of the importance of having a spouse with whom to share burdens and exchange encouragement.

Idea No. 2: The parenting roles of fathers and mothers are different.

In most cultures and marriages, parenting is fundamentally in the domain of the wife. [21] Men are usually much less involved than women in the daily care and supervision of the children, [22] and they tend to see themselves as part of a cast in a supporting role where their responsibility is to provide assistance to the primary parent, the mother.

The parenting activities of the husband tend to center around playing with the child and enforcing discipline. From the time the child is born, mothers are likely to assume more care giving responsibilities, even if the fathers are home and are free to help. [23] Fathers, on the other hand, are more likely to engage in active and stimulating play. [24] As the child grows older, the mother's role of primary care giver and the father's role of playmate generally continue.

A number of studies show that men and women find different roles in child rearing. [25] Women are found to be more nurturing, and men to focus more on their role of being the provider. Miller, [26] in her book *New Psychology of Women*, describes the role of the mother as the main nurturer:

If we look at what women have been doing in life, we see that a large part of it can be called active participation in the development of others. [27]

The mother's role has been described as an inescapable part of a mother's existence. [28] Men, of course, do experience part of the reproductive, nurturing, and childbearing roles but not at the same level and intensity as women.

Idea No. 3: Research shows more cultures report the majority of parenting activities are done by women.

Most of the studies about parenting roles are done in the USA. In our study mentioned earlier, we asked about men and women's roles in nine different cultures. Parents were asked two questions. The first question was, "How important was your spouse in meeting your parenting responsibilities?" There were three categories of possible answers: Not helpful, somewhat helpful, or extremely helpful. The second question was, "Give a percentage of the things that you did and the things your spouse was more responsible for".

Respondents were given eighteen activities to evaluate. We found that the spouse was considered extremely helpful across cultures and gender as seen in the table below.

TABLE 8.1

What They Said	Not Helpful	Somewhat Helpful	Extremely Helpful
Mothers	4%	26%	70%
Fathers	1%	7%	92%
Combined Male and Female	3%	17%	80%

*Chi Square = 18.07 (df = 2, n = 235) p = .000

Looking at Table 9.1, it is clear that mothers do more of these activities than do fathers, but the father still plays a large role as seen in Table 8.2.

TABLE 8.2

Percentage of Mothers and Fathers Who Selected a Response Category for Each Dependent Variable

Activity	More Father	Equal	More Father	Mostly Mother
Hugs and kisses	6%	37%	35%	22%
Explaining things	20%	45%	24%	12%
Teaching	13%	49%	31%	9%
Disciplining	35%	37%	18%	11%
Organizing	17%	31%	36%	19%
Helping with friends	9%	38%	36%	18%
Feeding	5%	20%	39%	38%
Getting ready for bed	7%	23%	41%	32%
Playing	25%	51%	17%	7%
Transportation	26%	35%	27%	13%
Joking around	40%	46%	9%	5%
Watching TV	45%	42%	9%	4%
Reading	17%	50%	21%	9%
Finances	51%	25%	13%	11%
Setting limits	33%	40%	18%	8%
Housekeeping	3%	15%	38%	44%
Cooking	4%	17%	76%	42%

*For this variable there was a significant Chi-Square at or beyond the p=.01 level of significance for gender.

**For this variable there was a significant Chi-Square at or beyond the p-.01 level of significance for cultures.

Idea No. 4: A parent's efforts and sacrifice for children show character.

The finding of this study suggested that women do more of the activities involved in parenting in all cultures studied. However, sometimes fathers do more than mothers do under special conditions such as if the work requires more physical labor. The large numbers in the "About Equal" category suggest that fathers can more considerably in the direction of being more active in what Jensen and Kingston 27 call the supporting cast. It is when special circumstances require more help and/or assistance that the manpower reserve is called in. In a changing culture, such as seen in the modernized industrialized nation with numerous social problems attributed to poor parenting, it would seem desirable to have elastic or permeable boundaries in sex roles so that fathers could move in and meaningfully contribute to the parenting responsibilities. The following example illustrates how two parents with different roles each worked for their children:

It always impressed me to see my mother dress up in her finest Sunday clothes, shiny makeup, and perfume to go visit my teachers at Parent Teacher Conferences. It was her way of showing the high value she placed on her children. My teachers loved the visits with my mother (as I always got a report the following school day). Each time they would comment on her southern accent and delightful spirit. One teacher said, "she got whooshed right in and whooshed right out."

She could have just run down in her grubbies, smelling like fried chicken, with no makeup on. But instead, she took the time to make a statement about her attitude, her character. I must have meant a lot to her. She was never nonchalant about her children. Mama left no question in anyone's mind about how she revered her own kids. That's character.

When my brother wanted a new pair of pants that we couldn't afford, Daddy went without lunch for a week, working hard physical labor in the hot sun in order to save enough. Sacrifice also shows character.

My parents' honesty and integrity has only been stronger since becoming parents. I believe that parenting pulls a lot of things out of you that you probably didn't even know existed. And, I think that if you allow it, parenting can truly enhance your character.

Idea No. 5: The roles of fathers and mothers are very diversified.

A student in our parenting class listed the things he had seen his parents do. The list was a mixture of serious and humorous items:

Nurse	Emergency medical technician
Coach	Entertainment planner
Financial controller	Comedian
Spiritual leader	Secretary
Warden	Truancy Officer
	Child Production
Cook	Janitor—to answer all deep
Cooking instructor	Purchasing agent

Fashion Coordinator	Philosopher-to answer the deep
Referee	questions
Taxi driver	Detective-to solve those difficult
Teacher—music,	reading, etc. mysteries
Boss-marketing expert	Diplomat-to improve Neighborhood
Consultant	relations

Now, to focus on your life as a parent and also that of your spouse, complete Learning Experience 8.1.

LEARNING EXPERIENCE 8.1

Parenting Tasks for Fathers and Mothers

As you read each of the activities listed below, check the response that most clearly describes by whom and to what extent the activity will be accomplished.

Mother's Answers

Activity	More Father	Equal	More Mother	Mostly Mother
Hugs and kisses				
Explaining things				
Teaching				
Disciplining				
Organizing				
Helping with friends				
Feeding				
Getting ready for bed				
Playing				
Transportation				
Joking around				
Watching TV				
Reading				
Finances				
Setting limits				
Housekeeping				
Cooking				

Father's Answers

Activity	More Father	Equal	More Mother	Mostly Mother
Hugs and kisses				
Explaining things				
Teaching				
Disciplining				
Organizing				
Helping with friends				
Feeding				
Getting ready for bed				
Playing				
Transportation				
Joking around				
Watching TV				
Reading				
Finances				
Setting limits				
Housekeeping				
Cooking				

I Other (fill in)

Principle 9

How to become more than the head of the house

Now that I have become a parent, I am starting to understand the importance of always putting my child's needs before my own. One example of this concept is that my wife's need and my need for sleep come second to my son's need for a bottle or a diaper change at three o'clock in the morning. Even though I will be tired for my classes the next day, nothing comes before my son.

In our study of the nine cultures, surveys were sent to parents, and they were asked to compare the mother and father in their homes using the following questions:

Who was the head of the house?

Who was in charge of what the children do?

Who was loved by the children?

Who was respected by the children?

Whose opinion was valued more?

Did children's needs come first?

They reflect the general agreement level or consistency across gender and across cultural studies when they answered these questions.

Idea No. 1: Research shows that fathers are still seen as the head of the household, but father and mother are seen as "about equal" in love, respect, and opinion valued by their children.

Our research of parents' opinions regarding family leadership revealed that nearly two-thirds (64 percent) regard fathers as the head of the house. Only 4 percent described mothers as head of the house and about one-third (32 percent) said fathers and mothers are about equal.

On the other hand, the same research showed that even though fathers are regarded as the head of the house, mothers are more likely to be in charge of what children actually do. For example, 30 percent of the respondents said that mothers are more in charge of what children do while only 9 percent attributed this responsibility to fathers. In response to the item about who is loved more by children, less than 1 percent named father and 13 percent named mother. Most of the children (87 percent) said children loved mother and father equally.

The next two items "respected by children" and "opinion valued more", are viewed as being about equal. Regarding who is respected by the children, most responded that both parents were respected equally by the children (80 percent). For the last item, it is clear that 94 percent agree that children's needs come first in the home, with only 6 percent disagreeing. Likewise, most respondents (67 percent) said that fathers' and mothers' opinions were valued about equally. These conclusions mentioned in Table 8.1 hold true across cultures and reflect the opinions of both men and women. It appears that mothers, in terms of behavior, are actually more in charge. So being the head of the house is not a designation to identify who is actually the one in charge of what children do. Nor does it mean that one is loved or respected more.

These findings present a rather clear answer to a question presented in the introduction. Being head of house does not translate into being more respected, loved, or valued.

Idea No. 2: The role of head of house is not a title or position of power but a role requiring sacrifice.

In my parents' household, the same was true when I was growing up. An example is when my father's job required that our family move to Japan. My father found out that we needed to move in January, which meant that he had a choice to make. He could either move my brother and me to a new school in a foreign country in the middle of the school year—from a school we had been in less than a year already—or he could make the preparations for us to move and start his job over in Japan and come back to the U.S. every couple of weeks.

The second option was obviously the less attractive option for my Dad, but he felt that it was important for my brother and me to finvwzish the school year in the place where we had started it. He knew that it was hard enough for us to move to a new school that year, as we had several times before, and that it was important to let us stay in this school and not make us start over again mid-year. My dad sacrificed his own need for his family to move with him to Tokyo and instead made the trip home every couple weeks for about six months. Neither option was easy, but clearly my father had my brother and me in mind when he made the decision—just as my wife and I will always keep my son's needs in mind when we make decisions.

A most crucial question in parenting relates to whose needs come first. Although parents have needs for sleep and health in order to work and function effectively, the reality is that in a family, parents are in the role of protectors and must put the needs of their children first. So, the "head of household" translates into putting the father into a role relating to the external world rather than a director of internal affairs. The role of head of household, rather than being a position of power and self-fulfillment, actually requires putting family needs ahead of self. This is not a meaningless role or even an empty title, but it appears to be a necessary title for a meaningful role.

Idea No. 3: To have more respect and love from children, fathers should be more involved in the home.

The most important lesson to learn from this study is for the fathers. The title "head of house" is not nearly as valuable as being loved and respected. How can a man receive more of this kind of love and respect? The answer is simple: Do more of what your wife does with the children.

In a book by Jensen and Petersen there is a chapter entitled, "When Dad Won't Help, Mom Is Helpless." In that chapter they reported some reasons why husbands may not be helpful at home:

1. He may view housework as strictly a female's responsibility— a threat to his masculine stereotype.

2. He may be concerned that his help will interfere with his job as the breadwinner.

3. He may not know just what it is the woman wants him to do.

4. He may not feel his efforts in the home are supported or appreciated.

5. He may feel that he has no time to put into helping around the house.

6. He may not see the value of helping in the home.

Idea No. 4: Mothers and children should give more appreciation to fathers who assist with child care and parenting.

Some men are insecure about their self-image and may be simply following the role models portrayed for them on TV such as those of football players, commentators, politicians, or even criminals. Compared to these seemingly glamorous and exciting roles, parenting may seem to be less glamorous but, as any successful father will tell you, there is no more dynamic role than that of parenting.

Another reason men do not help in the home is that many men perceive housework as interfering with their role as breadwinner but experience has shown that when fathers are more involved at home they are actually better able to perform their work.

The reason for this is that they can concentrate totally on their work because they don't have to be distracted by the possibility of problems at home.

Jensen and Petersen stress the importance of giving appreciation to fathers who assist in child care and planning. If society does not value a man's time in the home, at least his wife and children should, and this needs to be expressed in as many ways as possible. The best way for a woman to help a man be a good father and to put parenting first in his life is to show appreciation to him for his involvement with the children no matter how modest that involvement may be.

Now that we have discussed the benefits that can accrue to a man by being more than just "head of the house", complete Learning Experience 9.1.

LEARNING EXPERIENCE 9.1

Planning on Father Becoming More than Head of the House

1. In the space below, write what being "head of household" means to you.

2. Next, list specific actions that will result in fathers becoming:

   a. More loved:

   b. More respected:

   c. More able to put children's needs first:

3. Now, list specific actions mothers can take to help fathers become more loved and respected by children.

SUMMARY

Instructions: Mark a if the statement is true and b if it is false.

1. There are only three good reasons for having children.

2. The reasons you have for having children will influence the way that you parent.

3. Having children brings adult status, but that also requires adult levels of unselfish concern for others.

4. The parenting roles of fathers and mothers are different.

5. To the question "How important was your spouse in supporting you in parenting responsibilities," males said that their wives were extremely helpful, but wives said that spouses were only somewhat helpful or not helpful.

6. The mothers performed almost all roles more than did fathers in the research.

7. In the research nearly two-thirds of the respondents said that fathers were the head of the house.

8. Even though fathers are described as head of the house, respondents said that mothers are more in charge of what children actually do.

9. Most parents put their own needs ahead of their children.

10. "When dad won't help, mother is helpless," is a phrase that is not accurate, and there are definite reasons why husbands may not help.

LESSON THREE

The Home Environment Needs Love

After you have successfully completed this lesson, you should be able to do the following:

1. Discuss the two main branches of a positive home climate: love and organization.

2. Describe how to create five dimensions of love in a family setting.

Principle 10

What should a good home provide?

We wish to present a simple and practical way of conceptualizing parenting that is cross-culturally valid. The important concept is that the home's social-emotional climate is the major influence on human growth.

Idea No. 1: The ideal home provides both love and organization.

We conceptualize the ideal home climate as consisting of two parts— love and organization as seen in Figure 10.1 below:

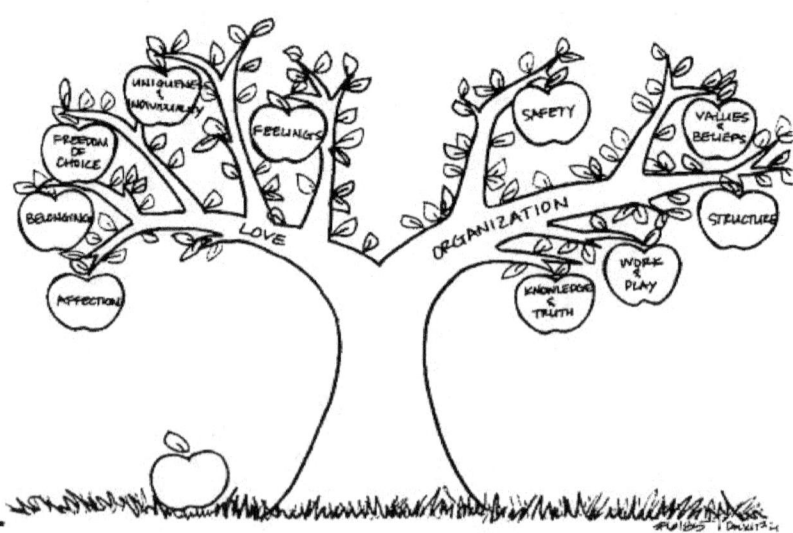

It is proposed that if the two basic elements of love and organization are present, children will naturally respond with positive behavior. Thus, always begin by trying to establish a positive growth climate in your home. The climate's two elements are love and organization.

Love consists of:

a climate with feelings

a climate with freedom and choice

a climate accepting of uniqueness and individuality demonstrated affection

a feeling of belonging

Idea No. 2: Love is given through feelings, freedom and choice, love and affection, belonging, and allowing individuality.

The first climate is that of feelings. Having more positive than negative emotions is the key for successful emotional learning. In addition to feelings, freedom of choice is second. In our view, love provides freedom and choice; humans flourish and grow when they are free to choose. Unfortunately, too many parents fear giving more freedom to children.

The third component of a loving environment is respecting each child's uniqueness and individuality. We see individuality as genetically determined and believe it is a mistake to try to mold children according to our preconceptions.

Affection is the fourth element. This need among children for physical comfort and affection is amply documented.

Finally, the fifth and last element is belonging. Each child needs an environment where he feels and knows he is accepted. In our culture, the family must provide this acceptance for optimal development.

The components of organization are:

a safe and nourishing physical climate

a climate with meaning which includes values and beliefs

knowledge and truth about world and self

work and play

structure

Idea No. 3: Organization is provided through climate, values, knowledge, work, and structure.

An accepting, warm climate is advocated—one in which the child is encouraged to experience feelings and to develop his own uniqueness through personal choice. Children must be provided with a predictable structure in which they feel safe. They must have expectations and guidelines placed upon them; they must be taught to contribute to the good of the family unit through efforts of their own; they must be able to derive meaning from what is going on around them, and to acquire knowledge about themselves and their surroundings.

In our opinion, if a positive psychological and social climate is provided, children will develop successfully, and an adjusted, well-balanced, and responsible person will emerge. Thus, it is proposed that when the ideal climate is provided, the need for more discipline and guidance will be minimized.

LEARNING EXPERIENCE 10.1

Providing Love and Organization in Our Homes

To complete your personal evaluation of the value of love and organization in the home, circle the appropriate answer to each of the following statements. **(KEY: SA=Strongly Agree; A=Agree; NS=Not Sure; D=Disagree; SD=Strongly Disagree)**

1. Children thrive best when there is little structure or few rules, so the children are able to set their own rules and make decisions themselves.

    SA   A   NS   D   SD

2. Part-time jobs and household chores are important to teach our children responsibility and the importance of working hard.

    SA   A   NS   D   SD

3. Children need a sense of belonging which comes from a home environment of acceptance.

    SA   A   NS   D   SD

4. Parents should not teach values and beliefs but let children discover these for themselves in the natural process of growing.

    SA   A   NS   D   SD

5. Children should be molded according to parents' preconceptions.

    SA   A   NS   D   SD

6. Optimal development of a child includes a safe and nourishing physical climate.

    SA   A   NS   D   SD

7. A predictable structure in the home makes the child feel safe.

    SA   A   NS   D   SD

8. Parents play a primary role in helping children acquire knowledge and truth about themselves and the world.

    SA   A   NS   D   SD

9. Children become stronger when they receive hugs and words of affection.

SA   A   NS   D   SD

10. Freedom is important but must be balanced with organization.

SA   A   NS   D   SD

TO SCORE: Questions 1 and 2: SA=5; A=4; NS=3; D=2; SD=1. Questions 3-5: SA=1; A=2; NS=3; D=4; SD=5. A high numerical score indicates you agree with the need for love and organization in the home.

LEARNING EXPERIENCE 10.2

To help you remember and be able to recall the components of love and organization, fill in the branches with the words used in Ideas 1 and 2. Be creative and colorful; it helps.

Principle 11

Love means showing affection.

Idea No. 1: Affection is a critical human need.

How important is it that children receive love? Well, maternity wards, after implementing "mother love" programs have shown decreases in infant mortality rates. In hospitals where much infant handling and affection occurs, the old, often fatal disease of marasmus is nonexistent. There is ample evidence that receiving love can well be a matter of life or death for many children.

Idea No. 2: Parent-child attachment develops in stages and is essential after seven months.

When do babies seek out their mothers? The early age at which infants seek their mothers is surprising. Schaffer and Emerson [29] studied the development of attachment in sixty Scottish infants for their first eighteen months of life. During the first two months of life, an infant requires affection constantly. By seven months the baby enters into "specific attachment." The infant begins to prefer a particular person and shows greater desire to be with this certain individual who is usually the mother. So actually at about the age of seven months the need to be with the mother is even stronger and separation from mother even more traumatic.

Idea No. 3: Infants and young children learn to show compassion by observing others in the family.

In one nine-month study, twenty-four mothers faithfully recorded their babies' actions and words in response to changes in emotional environment. [30] The mothers recorded their own responses as soon as possible after these events. The mothers were amazed to see how sensitive their babies were to people around them. Some babies as early as the age of one year actually tried to comfort people who cried in pain. They snuggled up to them, patted them, or hugged them, and sometimes tried to help them. One thirteen-month-old boy was busy eating his cereal when his tired father sat beside him, resting his head on his hand. The baby pulled the father's hand away and tried to feed him cereal.

Idea No. 4: Mother's warmth is a key factor for effective parenting.

Discussed elsewhere in this text is the study initiated by Robert Sears, Eleanor Maccoby, and Harry Levin. [31] They sought to identify parenting techniques that influence personality development by interviewing 379 mothers of kindergartners and rating each mother on 150 different child-rearing practices.

Twenty-five years later, David C. McClelland interviewed and tested many of those children who were then 31 years old, most with children of their own. McClelland and others concluded that practices such as breast-feeding, toilet training, and spanking were not all that important. How parents "feel" about their children made the difference. "'Mother's warmth' was found to be the key determinant of adult maturity. For example, it mattered whether a mother liked her child and enjoyed playing with the child or whether she considered the child a nuisance with negative characteristics. And, children of affectionate fathers were more likely to show tolerance and understanding than were children of other fathers." [32]

A student made the following statement, illustrating this type of parent, in a parenting class:

There were many times I didn't understand my father. And, although he never told me, I knew he loved me. How? He spent time with me and seemed to enjoy it. He carried me around a lot, put his arm around me, kissed me good night. I decided at a young age he enjoyed being a dad.

Contrast the above with the less fortunate story below:

My mother was an overworked woman with several children and didn't seem to enjoy any of us. She complained a lot, spanked, and slapped us around daily and made comments such as "Maybe when you kids are grown, I'll be able to have nice things again."

Idea No. 5: Discipline often is unnecessary when love is felt.

Some psychologists say that ignoring inappropriate behavior extinguishes it. We believe, however, that there is a better approach. That approach is to take time to hold, rock, or speak affectionately to a child. Love can be expressed even in discipline.

My father would always take us aside into another room and in a silent manner give us a hug and smile which were always so soft and tender. This form of love and affection would always satisfy my needs and change my whole attitude toward helping my parents. It is really surprising what two or three minutes alone with your father can do. Not only was his love demonstrated through his tender hugs, but as I grew older these experiences taught me that the giving of time is a great expression of love and that words aren't always necessary for demonstrating love. This experience has affected my adolescent and adult life, enabling me to be more sensitive and empathetic toward others.

A babysitter solved a problem by showing affection.

One summer afternoon I was babysitting a few children. One of them was a little boy about two-years-old. He was a calm child and I had never seen him throw a fit. One of his mother's rules was that the kids weren't supposed to go outside without their sandals. Well, he went outside barefooted and I called him back in to put on his sandals. He started to stomp around and cry, saying that he didn't want to wear them. At first I tried to explain why he needed to put them on but it was obvious that he wasn't listening. So I picked him up and held him gently until he calmed down. Then, after he was calm I asked him if he wanted to put his sandals on and go outside, and he said "Yes." I put his sandals on him and he jumped up and ran outside to play, all carefree and happy like two-year-olds are supposed to be and like he usually was.

Idea No. 6: Giving love to our children can also help solve other problems such as sibling rivalry.

It may be surprising, but giving love oftentimes cuts down on the time demanded by young children. A mother, after having twins, was experiencing difficulties with her two older children.

Erik, eight years old, demands equal time, of course, and the evenings I'm not with Douglas, Erik and I have our turn. His requests include long conversations, scripture stories, and working out problems he encounters with school work or playmates at school. I have also found this to be an ideal time to introduce books and discussions about the "birds and the bees." Erik has cut down on his constant demands for my attention because he is sure his turn will come.

Idea No. 7: Fathers can play an important part in communicating love to their children.

Can men be as nurturing and loving as women in caring for their offspring? In their own way they can. Men have the potential to be good caretakers. Parke and Sawin [33] observed the behavior of both middle- and lower-class parents of newborns in hospital maternity wards and concluded that fathers are just as responsive as mothers to their infant's vocalizations and movements. Fathers touch, look at, talk to, rock, and kiss babies in much the same way as mothers. But, while the fathers are more likely to talk to babies, mothers are likely to touch more. Fathers are just as protective and giving as mothers, and even more likely than mothers to hold and look at their babies, although mothers smiled at their babies more. The researchers concluded that fathers and mothers are not interchangeable. Each contributes to the needs of the child in a unique way.

How deep love can be and a student in a parenting class touchingly expressed how vital it is even during later childhood:

Then my father looked at me and said he loved me. He had never said that to me before and I didn't know quite how to react, but inside it changed me and my attitude toward my father. Somehow I was able to see a part of him that craved the same love and affection as I. He told me I was valuable to him and that I had many capabilities. I knew then that I was worthwhile. I really believe that experience is what caused me to get better grades in school and to improve my social functioning. It only took that simple phrase, "I love you."

Idea No. 8: The best ways of communicating love and affection depend on the age of the child.

There are possibly as many specific ways of communicating love and affection as there are parents and children. For the young child, love and affection may be shown by verbal expressions, hugging, kissing, holding, rocking, tousling hair, spending time playing, singing, talking, etc.

As the child becomes older, however, he may begin to be embarrassed by open displays of affection. However, the child still needs to know he is loved. This can be expressed in words during moments of closeness which should be arranged by the parent as often as possible. For older children a quick squeeze in passing, rumpling of the hair or a pat on the shoulder can be effective. For this age group, showing love means spending quality time with the child, respecting the child, expressing positive feelings about the child, and giving positive feedback.

Idea No. 9: Love the child even if you cannot and should not love the behavior.

Parents need to show love and affection regardless of the child's achievements; a child needs to feel valued apart from his accomplishments. He needs to feel loved for who he is not what he does. Whenever personal worth is dependent upon performance, personal value is subject to cancellation with every wrong step. Also, if the child's personal worth is dependent upon performance, an unhealthy attitude of competition results. Parents need to separate the child's performance from the child himself; love the child even if you cannot love the improper behavior.

Principle 12

Love means providing freedom and choice.

The decision I faced was the choice of going on a mission for my church or continuing school with a basketball scholarship. I approached my father on this matter, knowing that he favored my basketball career over serving a mission. Needless to say, I was impressed by the way he handled the situation. . . . As we sat together, he made a list of the positive consequences of each choice and a list of the negative ones. After acting as my counselor, my father gave me the lists and left the final decision to me. He had discussed his experiences and shared his knowledge, which gave me a greater insight into my own choices. Yet, I never felt pressured by him to respond one way or another. He realized that I needed to be satisfied and happy with my choice in order to succeed in the direction I chose to go. After reviewing the pros and cons we had drawn up, I chose to go on a mission at that time in my life.

Idea No. 1: Making choices benefits children whether young or older.

Sometimes the element of growth comes from actually making the choice, since it is making the choice itself which is more important than what the choice is. We learn by facing choices and trying to understand their consequences. The growth this young person realized, being able to freely make a decision, is not limited to just older children. Decision-making can benefit even small children. One mother would pick out three outfits and then give her two-and-a-half-year-old child freedom to choose one of the three outfits. As the child grew older he learned more about clothing and how to dress, but more importantly he was learning how to make decisions.

Idea No. 2: Research indicates that moderate levels of freedom and control are best.

How necessary to psychological development is the freedom to act for oneself? Is there evidence supporting or refuting the notion that we must experience freedom in order to effectively progress?

Though the question is general, we argue that for healthy psychological development there must be controlled freedom, and that the most critical time for humans to experience controlled freedom of choice is early childhood.

Because each child is unique, roles are interpreted differently by each set of parents thus there is no single approach to proper parental control. Restrictive parents interfere with independence. Restrictiveness can lead to fearful, dependent, and submissive behaviors on one hand and on the other it can lead to rebellion and disobedience.

Diana Baumrind, [34] was interested in the difference between children raised in authoritarian (restrictive), authoritative, and permissive homes. Authoritarian parents attempt to shape, control, and evaluate the child's behavior with strict rules and requirements. Unquestioned obedience is stressed, forceful discipline preferred, and verbal give- and-take discouraged. Baumrind's findings showed that children raised in this type of home were discontented, withdrawn, and highly distrustful. These children also had high anxiety and fear levels.

Permissive parents were non-punitive and accepting. However, when children were allowed total autonomy in regulating their own behavior, Baumrind found that these children lacked self-reliance, self-control, and exploratory behaviors. They had a high level of indecision and uncertainty.[43]

When Baumrind studied the third category of parents—the authoritative—she found that parents in this category provided firm direction but gave children considerable freedom. This freedom had certain limits, however, which were agreed upon by both parent and child.

Parental control was not rigid, intrusive, or unnecessarily restrictive. Reasons were given for family policies, and there was a high amount of verbal give and take. There was concerned response to children's wishes and needs. The results of this study found that children raised in the authoritative home were self-reliant, self-controlled, explorative, and contented. They were also able to develop a strong interpersonal competency. [35]

Idea No. 3: If parents allow the child to make decisions they should support those decisions. Otherwise, parents should tell children if they cannot support a decision.

While the exact mixture of permissiveness and restrictiveness cannot be prescribed, a general rule might be to provide the child with as much freedom as possible, while at the same time monitoring the child's behavior so that it stays within the limits of acceptability. Providing freedom of choice involves genuineness. If honesty or genuineness in providing freedom of choice are absent, the benefits of providing this opportunity for responsibility may not be realized. One student recalled having to make the decision of whether to go home or stay at a university:

I had called home almost every night crying and feeling really down. I told my mom and dad I was thinking about coming home but what I really wanted was for them to just say, "Come on home." My parents told me they would be supportive if I made my own decision. Well, within the next few days I had sold my contract, withdrawn from school, and booked a flight home for the following week. That night I called home to tell my parents what I had decided to do. When I told my mom I had withdrawn from school and booked a flight home, all she said was, "Karen, you didn't!" in a disappointed tone. I was so upset after she had said that. I felt like I had really disappointed her and let her down. After I had gone home she didn't ever say anything negative about my decision again but her initial reaction spoke louder than anything. The thing I want to stress is that parents, after letting the child make his/her own decision, should support the child.

The above example reveals the importance of genuine approval of a child's decision. If approval cannot be given, the parent should be honest and open about that hesitancy. In essence, if the parent is going to allow the child to make the decision, then the parent must be prepared to accept whatever that decision may be "no strings attached." The time for the parent to express concerns or disagreement with a pending decision is before granting the child the option of making the decision.

To summarize, a home environment with freedom benefits a child's psychological development. This is *not* a recommendation for permissiveness—that bounds, limits, or consequences should be removed. A climate with a balance between freedom and organization will be discussed later.

Now turn to Learning Experience 12.1 to test your understanding of the concepts and to Learning Experience 12.2 for a self-evaluation.

LEARNING EXPERIENCE 12.1

Allowing Children Freedom of Choice

In the space provided before each statement, write either T if you believe the statement to be true or F if you believe the statement to be false. True answers indicate this statement to be the best choice for allowing freedom of choice; false identifies the statement of an attitude that is too controlling or gives too much freedom of choice.

_____I avoid influencing my child's decision-making because it is his or her life to make it or break it.

_____Older children should be given more freedom to make choices than should younger children.

_____Children should be allowed total autonomy in regulating their own behavior.

_____Children should always obey without question, and forceful discipline should be administered if they do not obey.

_____If the parent cannot accept the child's decision, it is better not to let the child make the decision in the first place.

_____It is better to give full freedom at a very young age so children learn to make their own life choices early.

_____Parents should allow the child the freedom to make major decisions even though the parent may not like the decision.

_____Children should be given considerable freedom within limits that are agreed upon by parents and child.

_____Parents should support the child's decision if they allow him or her to make the decision and if a negative choice does not have long-term costs.

_____Children's behavior should be monitored so that it stays within the limits of socially-acceptable behavior.

_____I try to give my child two or more acceptable choices and then let him/her make the final decision.

LEARNING EXPERIENCE 12.2

Self-Evaluation of Parenting Styles

Baumrind distinguished three types of homes (authoritarian, authoritative, and permissive). To determine which type of home you would establish or have at this time, circle the appropriate response to each statement.

(KEY: SA=Strongly Agree; A=Agree; NS=Not Sure; D=Disagree; SD=Strongly Disagree)

1. Children need to learn unquestioning obedience at an early age.

   SA   A   NS   D   SD

2. Children should make most of their own decisions at early ages since they are the ones who must live with the consequences of those decisions.

   SA   A   NS   D   SD

3. Parents should give firm direction in their children's lives by not be rigidly controlling.

   SA   A   NS   D   SD

4. Children should learn to regulate their own behavior by getting to choose whatever they want to do.

   SA   A   NS   D   SD

5. Parents should strive to be totally accepting and nonjudgmental about their children's behavior.

   SA   A   NS   D   SD

6. Children should not take part in setting rules in the family; they will be able to run their own families when the time comes.

   SA   A   NS   D   SD

7. Verbal give-and-take between parents and children is very helpful for setting family policies.

   SA   A   NS   D   SD

8. Forceful discipline is necessary to make children abide strictly to parental rules and requirements.

SA   A   NS   D   SD

9. Parents should give children considerable freedom within limits agreed upon by parents and children.

SA   A   NS   D   SD

10. Verbal give-and-take between parents and children is often disrespectful and is really just "talking back."

SA   A   NS   D   SD

Evaluation of Scores:

1. If you answered "SA" or "A" to two or more of the following: #1, #6, #8, #10, the style of parenting you would probably implement would be *Authoritarian.*

2. If you answered "SA" or "A" to two or more of the following: #2, #4, #5, the style of parenting you would probably implement would be *Permissive.*

3. If you answered "SA" or "A" to two or more of the following: #3, #7, #9, the style of parenting you would probably implement would be *Authoritative.*

Principle 13

Love means respect for individuality and uniqueness.

I grew up with a girl whose father was very restrictive. He was a minister. As far as I can remember, Julie seldom got to make a real decision about anything she did. It seems her father always decided when she could go anywhere, when she was to return, who she went with, and even how she got there. Her father had to be consulted on everything that went on in her life and then he made the decisions for her.

Idea No. 1: Children like to be special just like all people do.

During childhood most of us remember wanting to be *best* in something. By adulthood, most people find this dream impossible. However, the psychological search continues. We like people who treat us special. Most people like to be called by their first name and even find they can laugh at and take pride in their individual differences. Underlying this peculiar human quality is the nature of man to seek for himself, to become his true self.

Idea No. 2: Most people have a strong desire to be unique.

Psychology has a subdiscipline called "individual differences." Textbooks written on this subject repeatedly point out the uniqueness and individuality of each human. Geneticists show that being alike is only possible in those rare cases of identical twins, and even then, differences still exist. Those acquainted with identical twins often find that the twins seek to be different.

Idea No. 3: Parents should allow children to pursue their own interests and to be individuals.

The positive climate, respecting individuality and uniqueness, does not endorse being different for difference's sake; rather, it emphasizes that individuality is natural and must be respected. It is difficult to ascertain why we seek uniqueness and individuality.

Perhaps from the beginning, biological differences provide an impetus in this direction. Even at birth, distinct differences exist among infants. [36] Thomas, Chess, and Birch found that 40 percent of infants studied were classified as easy to warm up to, 15 percent slow to warm up to, 10 percent difficult, and 35 percent inconsistent. Follow-up studies at five and ten years showed the continuance of these traits and it is suggested that they may also continue into adulthood. [37]

Our desire to be treated uniquely and as individuals may stem from a knowledge that each of us is different. Even though man is classified and treated as member of a group, this classification process is not congruent with the inherent knowledge that he is different. To accept anonymity would be like living a lie. The knowledge that we will not behave and respond precisely as predicted, demanded, or expected is interpreted as our rebelling against being grouped or "pigeonholed". We do not want to be someone else so we do what is necessary to avoid the artificiality of being classified. A healthy social environment allows and accepts individuality. One example of this type of environment in a family setting was related by a young girl who described the relationship between her brother and her father:

My brother is not the kind of son my father had hoped to have. My father was interested in athletics, the outdoors, etc., but my brother was interested and talented in the field of art. My father wanted a son he would be able to do things with, but he knew that my brother's interests didn't coincide with his, and Father didn't push the issue. He had respect for my brother and his talents and encouraged him to develop them. Father often said that he wanted for us what we wanted for ourselves. My brother, my sister, and I are very different from each other and my father taught us that there was nothing wrong with that difference. My parents allowed each of us to become separate individuals with our own identities, which in turn gave us confidence in ourselves.

Idea No. 4: Adolescence is a time of searching for identity.

Erik Erickson pointed out that adolescents universally face a developmental task of searching for identity. One girl, going through this identity search, deliberately attempted to be an individual during the ninth grade:

Throughout grade school and most of junior high, I was always trying to be someone else. Of course, the person I was trying to be was always the most popular girl because popular girls seemed to be having all the fun. By the ninth grade, I had decided that these girls were all the same. None of them had their own personality. They talked, dressed, ate, sang, and walked the same, at the same time, and in the same places. Suddenly, I wanted to be me—Rebecca—my own person. Who was I? What was I like? I was determined to find out.

Idea No. 5: Nurture the biological uniqueness inherent in every child.

Unfortunately, in some family situations the emphasis on meeting expectations and belonging to the group often forces a conformity on a child that is not only undesirable but also unhealthy. For example, parents often want their children to have opportunities and advantages that they missed, or to meet potentials that they regret not attaining themselves. If a mother never had the opportunity to take piano lessons, or frittered away the opportunity when she had the chance as a child or adolescent, she may force lessons on her daughter because she regrets her past decisions. Perhaps a father who never met his potential sees in his son a way of extending himself. Unfortunately, forcing the parent's personality upon the child is rarely successful and more often than not results in frustration and rebellion. When children's true selves are not accepted and they are forced into roles in which they do not fit, the result is frequently low self-esteem. This is reflected in self-esteem tests where items such as "I often wish I were someone else" are marked as an indication of the way the child feels about himself.

Following is a good example of emphasis on individuality, which was expressed by a girl:

When I was growing up, individuality was emphasized more than conformity in my family. Although my parents did not particularly try to be nonconformists, our lifestyle was very different from that of other families we knew. My parents placed considerable emphasis on helping us develop our own unique talents and abilities. As a result, I accepted my parents' unstated but implicit values.

Now turn to Learning Experience 13.1 to see if you can determine which influences and circumstances contribute to individuality and uniqueness and which ones encourage conformity or sameness.

LEARNING EXPERIENCE 13.2

One of the ways in which your life as a parent or teacher or leader may be more pleasant is determined by whether you believe each person should be unique and different from others. Circle the number which most accurately states your actions or feelings.

ANSWER KEY: 0=Never; 1=Sometimes; 2=Most of the time; 3=Always.

0 1 2 3   I call people by their names whenever possible.

0 1 2 3   I think twins should be treated as individuals and not be forced to wear matching clothes, etc.

0 1 2 3   In dealing with children from the same family I try to treat each one differently.

0 1 2 3   I think newborns come with differences in personality.

0 1 2 3   As a parent I try (or will try) not to force or coerce my son or daughter into engaging in the activities that only I think best.

0 1 2 3   I encourage others to seek their own identities and to be themselves.

0 1 2 3   I think it is important to include children in goal-setting for their own lives in order that they can express their own unique potential.

0 1 2 3   The search for identity is an important part of an adolescent's task of reaching maturity.

0 1 2 3   I try to help adolescents find their own identities.

0 1 2 3   I believe that the ideal family climate encourages the uniqueness of each child.

Principle 14

Love means having feelings.

As a child I was raised in a loving home. That's not to say there were never any displays of negative feelings—there were. I remember Mom and Dad disagreeing about things, but I was also able to see them work things out and be happy again. This helped me in many ways. It showed me that people could have problems and still work them out. It also helped me to know I could go to my folks for help to handle my own feelings if I was upset or didn't understand. I feel that I was better prepared to deal with my own feelings and interactions with others later in life because of this environment.

Idea No. 1: Home is a place to learn to handle feelings—both positive and negative.

This student insightfully noticed that negative as well as positive feelings could exist in a happy home. Here is another fact about feelings: they can be dangerous. Uncontrolled anger, rage, or hate have literally ruined the lives of potentially happy people.[38] While these violent, high-energy emotions are obviously dangerous, less visible emotions of depression, despair, and anguish are equally destructive. It was wise for the student above to know that in his family, he had the opportunity to learn to handle feelings so that they did not ruin his life.

Idea No. 2: Home should be a place for the child to handle difficult feelings.

While the home climate must present opportunities for children to handle and experience a wide range of emotions, it can also be a safe place to shelter a child from difficult feelings. Rejected and frightened children return home, run to their parents, and find security. Home provides a safe haven from frightening, disintegrating emotions, not only for the young child, but also for the older child and adolescent.

Idea No. 3: Parents should avoid forcing children to suppress all negative feelings.

Children will inevitably feel a variety of emotions in their lives. The helpful climate is one in which even negative, embarrassing, or personal feelings can be expressed and openly confronted. Suppressing or hiding these feelings provides no service to the child who must deal with the feelings inwardly on his own, often keeping them inside and producing anxiety.

As good as my father is, there were times when I had very strong negative feelings toward some of the things he expected of me. He would not allow the expression of my feelings on his "word" in any way. Because of this fact, I have bottled up a few harsh feelings for him. These do not get in the way of my love for him, but they do get in the way of having fond memories. I also tend to hold back expressions of any sort—good or bad. I feel that by expressing some negative feelings earlier in my life, I would have been able to work things out with my father.

Idea No. 4: People having negative feelings can still be happy if there are more positive than negative feelings.

A third important concern regarding emotions is the type of emotion. More positive than negative emotions should be present for optimal psychological development.

This means that a person having many negative feelings in his life will still report being happy if negative feelings are outweighed by a large number of positive feelings. In a later study, Bradburn38 used a test called the Affect Balance Scale, to measure psychological well being as the difference between scores on positive and negative feeling items. Interestingly, they found that people who reported experiencing many positive feelings were not happier than those who reported fewer. It was the proportion of positive to negative feelings that determined happiness. The presence of positive emotions was correlated with social involvement and new and varied experiences.

Emotions such as hate, anger, resentment, rage, and jealousy cannot be shown to be helpful or beneficial. At best, they are inevitable and must be dealt with but are clearly undesirable. On the other hand, positive emotions enhance a child's development and personal-social adjustment.

Idea No. 5: The child growing up with positive emotions in the home is more likely to be a happy child.

One prominent child psychologist writes in her text, "If a child grows up in a home environment where happiness prevails and where friction, animosity, jealousy, and other unpleasant emotional experiences are kept to a minimum, the chances are that he will become a happy child". [39]

Now proceed to Learning Experience 14.1 to test your recall of the concepts presented.

LEARNING EXPERIENCE 14.1

Love Means Having Feelings and Emotions

Fill in the blanks in each of the following statements.

1. Emotions include positive and _____ feelings.

2. Some emotions are safe while others are _____ .

3. Home is a place where a child should be able to express a _____ range of emotions.

4. Home should be a place to learn to handle and _____ frightening and overwhelming emotions.

5. Avoid high levels of stress and _____ in the life of the young child.

6. Some parents go to extremes and deny _____ in themselves and will not allow children to express their _____ either.

7. Forcing the child to hide or suppress feelings may cause him to turn such feelings as _____ .

8. Neurotic symptoms begin at the point that the child cannot recognize his feelings and emotions and they have moved into the _____ .

9. Optimal psychological development requires more _____ than _____ .

10. Happiness seems to depend on the relative balance of one's _____ .

Idea No. 5: (Respond to this idea by telling why it is true) the child growing up with positive emotions is more likely to be a happy child.

Principle 15

Love means providing a sense of belonging.

Idea No. 1: There are many social practices that help humans feel they belong.

Idea No. 2: Belonging to a family is very important to a child.

Besides the innate striving to belong, there are many social customs that sustain group membership. Family names are often used to help a child be aware of his belonging--"I'm an Adams." Formal membership often begins even in children's neighborhood clubs. Perhaps more important than names and formal membership are informal activities such as participating in decisions, sharing of resources and time, and assuming group responsibility. These actions cause a person to feel secure and to belong. To show how she became more closely tied with a feeling of family membership, one student related the following:

In our family we all "belong" to each other very much. I would say that the main reason for this feeling is that we were often given the opportunity to contribute to family functioning. An example of this opportunity that we had while we were growing up concerns our many financial difficulties. Of course, it was my father's basic responsibility to provide for our family, but there were many hard times when my father's paycheck just didn't cover everything. My parents called us together and asked us to contribute all our savings into a family "pot." It made us feel very much a part of a good cause—our survival. We felt that everything we had was "ours," not "mine." We had to get together and work for the welfare of our family and it brought us closer together. My parents felt that there was nothing dishonorable about asking us, the children, to help out during difficult times.

Conditions making the family important to a child may be seen by others as having little value.

The family is, however, the child's first primary group and despite voices to the contrary, the family still seems to be the most prevailing, enduring, primary group. A sense of belonging to this group is important to a child.

Idea No. 3: There are many things both mothers and fathers can do to help children feel like they belong.

Some parents give considerable time and effort to activities that cement a group feeling of solidarity. The enduring results of this type of effort were explained in this way:

They shared time with us in many ways, but in my case, two things left a great impression on me. First, my mother would read to me. As a result, I am an avid reader today and enjoy a closeness of interests with my mother in the things we read. Second, my father practiced all kinds of sports with me, whatever I happened to be interested in at the time. We went through swimming, basketball, baseball, football, boxing, and trap and skeet shooting. As a result, I am interested in most sports and enjoy a closeness with my father.

Idea No. 4: Children without a strong family may have unique needs for belonging.

In a parenting class, a mother described her efforts to produce a feeling of belonging between her new husband and her son so that the stepfather/son relationship would sustain a feeling of belonging. She said:

My son and I were alone for six years. I remarried and my husband is now part of this family unit and we are expecting a new baby this summer. It has been hard for my son to accept this new arrangement and find where he belongs. I think much of his misbehavior stems from the need to belong.

There is a soundness in this mother's theory. Being involved in sharing problems and helping to establish and maintain rules have been shown by researchers to be important in the acceptance of rules and the attitude toward them.40 A feeling of not really belonging to a family group can be especially devastating to children, often resulting in an almost pathological seeking of membership. One such case was described as follows:

I had a girlfriend in high school who was really close to me. Her parents were divorced, she had stepbrothers and sisters, and home life was obviously unhappy. The contention got to be so bad that she dreaded the thought of returning home after school. She avoided her home as long as she could. This usually meant she would come home with me. She soon "adopted" us as her family and we began to see her as another member of our family. She ate with us, went on family activities with us, and even began doing chores around the house. She and my mother became quite close, and she even called her "Mom." She really did belong. For all intents and purposes she was a member of our family.

Idea No. 5: Parents often have special insight regarding meeting individual needs for a feeling of belonging.

Teachers and other adults working with children can relate countless examples of children who seek out other groups when they do not have strong family ties and a sense of belonging. It was fortunate for the child in the above example that the family she semi-adopted accepted her. Many children are not so lucky and often desperately cling to peer and childhood groups which are frequently neither stable nor supportive.

In other cases, some children have families and parents who strongly support children's needs as shown by the following example of how a transient family gave stability and support to a young child:

Our family moved to Tennessee where my younger brother, David, would be entering first grade. My brother was somewhat apprehensive at the thought of a new town, a new school, and the whole new experience of first grade. At his request, my mother would drive him to school and walk him to the door of his classroom every day. The principal told her she shouldn't do that any more. My mother replied, "He feels more comfortable if I just walk him to his class. It's a new and sometimes frightening experience for him." The principal told her that she would ruin him, that he would never be independent or outgoing. But this was my mother's sixth child and she decided she knew better than the principal how to handle her child.

The sense of belonging to a group is a necessity for optimal psychological development. Hopefully, the examples above provided illustrations of how to identify and develop this important part of a healthy psychological climate for the child.

Now proceed to Learning Experience 15.1.

LEARNING EXPERIENCE 15.1

Self-Test on Helping Children Gain a Sense of Belonging

ANSWER KEY: 0=Never; 1=Sometimes; 2=Usually; 3=Almost Always

0 1 2 3   Help my children live up to the norms and standards of our family and there by feel part of a close group—our family.

0 1 2 3   Help my children feel like they belong to our family by letting them plan and contribute to family activities.

0 1 2 3   Help my children feel like they belong by having family councils.

0 1 2 3   Be home as much as possible when children are home to help them feel like they *really* belong.

0 1 2 3   Read books to children to help them feel like they belong.

0 1 2 3   Have camping trips and similar type activities to help children feel close to family members.

0 1 2 3   Involve children in decision-making to help them feel like an important part of the family.

SUMMARY

Instructions: Mark *a* if the statement is true and *b* if it is false.

1. In the tree illustration it shows that love is the foundation, and that organization should be built on love.

2. Organization is provided through: 1) discipline, 2) family planning, 3) schedules, 4) financial security, and 5) daily exercise.

3. Affection is a critical human need.

4. A mother's warmth is a key factor in affective parenting.

5. When there is an abundance of love, discipline is often unnecessary and other problems are solved such as sibling rivalry.

6. Fathers can play an important role in communicating love to their children.

7. Research indicates that moderate levels of freedom and control are best.

8. While uniqueness and individuality is important for adults, it is not so important for children, as they like being similar to other children.

9. Adolescence is a time for searching for conformity.

10. In the home both positive and negative emotions should be allowed and expressed, but the majority should be positive.

LESSON FOUR

The Home Environment Needs Organization

After you have successfully completed this lesson, you should be able to do the following:

1. Define the five dimensions of an organized home environment.

2. Explain how to create the five dimensions of organization in a family setting.

Principle 16

An organized home has structure.

Idea No. 1: High expectations generally produce positive results.

I remember a time when my mother applied expectations to set limits on my behavior. I had begun to date and we were discussing the time I should be home. She said, "I'm not going to set a specific time for you to be home. You've always shown good judgment. I'm trusting you." I felt that I would rather break my neck than break her trust. If I were to abuse her trust, she would have to set a specific rule. I felt greater motivation to get home early by her trusting me than I would have with a rule.

Expectations, though similar to demands, are more conducive to the development of freedom and trust as seen in the above story.

Idea No. 2: High expectations help children set their own high standards of behavior.

Summarizing research about parents who establish definite expectations and have rules to insure compliance, psychologist Eleanor Maccoby states that children with this type of parent are low in aggression, altruistic rather than egotistic, and above average in competence and agency.

[41] On the other hand, low parental demands have been associated with high aggression, low impulse control, and immaturity.

Furthermore, Maccoby states that when parents consistently enforce rules and prevent their children from taking control, the children are better able to control aggressive impulses. She asserts that:

A demand is a goal that the child is expected to meet, and goals vary. Some parents expect help with their household tasks or child care, others demand politeness and consideration in interpersonal relationships. When parents make few demands, they may be underestimating the child's capacity and maturity level, or they may be so disinterested and preoccupied that they find it easier to do things themselves than to get the child to do them. The positive outcomes of high demands--especially a sense of competency--can only by expected if the child has the necessary skills to meet the demands. . . in other words, high parental demands that are appropriate to the child's age and are accompanied by training can provide a stepping stone to self-reliance.

Idea No. 3: Some parental demands may be destructive to the parent-child relationship and prevent children from pursuing their own worthwhile interests.

The power of a simple expectation is usually underestimated. On the other hand, the following story illustrates how restrictive demands may inhibit a child's growth:

My father always seemed to want me to be like him—I am the only boy in my family. One of the earliest experiences I remember (I was about seven) involved ice skating. In his youth, my father was a fine figure skater. As far back as I can remember he wanted me to enjoy it as much as he did, and to become as good or better than he had been. Unfortunately, I can't and never could, tolerate ice skating. I just don't like it.

My father never seemed able to understand or accept my feelings about ice skating. He would often make me go to the local rink, or arrange parties, thereby forcing me by social pressure to go. He gave me his old figure skates and, even though they didn't fit, I wore them to please him. They would hurt, but one particular night the pain was specially bad. When I got home, my dad saw my broken and bleeding blisters; he finally seemed to understand. After that he never pressured me about skating again.

Had this father continued with his demands, the child may have pursued a pastime from which he was deriving no pleasure, possibly preventing personal excellence in desired areas, and interfering with a positive father-son relationship.

Expectations, however, when accompanied by trust and freedom, will sometimes produce more growth than demands because individuals assume some responsibility for their personal actions.

This concept is expressed in the following:

As a child growing up, I wanted to meet these "expectations" because I wanted to please my parents, even though I did not feel pressure to act a certain way. I always knew I had the freedom to meet or not meet these expectations. The fact that they were implied and not hard and fast rules helped us kids experience individual responsibility and freedom to perform as we wished. Most of our actions, decisions, and behaviors were condoned and supported by our parents.

It is important to note that demands may be necessary at times. Some parental control is necessary for adequate development of self-control in the child.[42] however, that heavy reliance on unalterable demands may bring about temporary compliance but lead to increased anti-social behaviors when parents are not present.

Idea No. 4: Expectations should have three elements.

Often, adults do not know how to state expectations or establish rules. Simply stated, this practice involves (1) letting children know what is expected in advance; (2) giving them a chance to practice it; and (3) helping them understand the consequences. As will be discussed later, allowing the child to participate in establishing rules or expectations will result in greater success.

Idea No. 5: Social development requires that children learn to obey rules, use manners, and otherwise behave acceptably.

The total range of behavior can be included in rules, demands, and expectations. Some examples of reasonable expectations were given by a mother of several pre- and elementary school-age children:

My children know there is a difference between inside and outside play, and they are expected to act accordingly. Inside, they must play reasonably quiet games; no running or chasing is allowed. Outside, however, the sky is the limit as long as they play safely and don't disturb the neighbors.

They also realize that although good manners are expected at all mealtimes, eating in a restaurant requires extra effort. They know we use quieter voices and observe stricter table etiquette.

The kids have been taught that we give the same respect to other people's homes as we do to our own. When they are at a friend's house, they know to be just as polite and considerate of inside rules as they are at home. They have found that they are always welcome guests because they behave in an acceptable fashion.

Idea No. 6: Follow-through is an essential part of home organization.

Expectations will not be effective unless there is follow-through. Sometimes parents simply forget; other parents have so many things going on they are unable to notice, thus, neglecting to provide the necessary guidance. In the long run, these parents will have less time for their children, and will soon believe that simple expectations do not work. And, the children will believe that expectations are not important to the parent. One mother who has this same view states:

We have a family council whenever it seems necessary. My son has had real difficulty fulfilling his responsibilities at home and at school. We sat down in a council and talked to him about his feelings. He felt the problem was that he was lazy and had too many demands on him at school and at home. We negotiated at home and dropped one of his jobs. We talked to the teacher at school. Apparently, he was goofing off at school instead of doing his work. The other children were able to accomplish their work plus do extra, so there was no negotiation in this area. Each Friday we checked with his teacher and got a list of his homework. Expectations were made clear that if he caught up on his school work he had privileges to do specific activities he liked to do; if he wasn't caught up, the weekend meant school work.

In summary, it is necessary and beneficial to impose structure in the environment in the form of expectations and demands. These require follow-through and effort but assist the child in developing social maturity and acceptable behavior. It is felt that these expectations will not be resisted but actually welcomed by the child.

Idea No. 7: Sometimes adolescent children want their parents to set rules and make demands so the adolescent can avoid offending peers.

In some cases, children seek rules for help in their lives. Ironically, one teenage daughter called her father late at night from a party seeking an expectation from him. Her father was surprised to get her call as he was not expecting her home for some time. This is how the conversation went:

Daughter: "Dad, do I have to come home now?"

Father: "No, of course you don't."

Daughter: "Oh, Dad, why do I have to?"

Father: "You don't. I said you could stay late tonight."

Daughter: "Please, Dad, just this one time."

Father: "You want me to tell you to come home?"

Daughter: "Okay, I'll be right home."

Proceed to Learning Experience 16.1 to practice the concepts presented.

LEARNING EXPERIENCE 16.1

Accomplishing Goals through Rules, Demands, and Expectations

In the following activity, write or imagine a rule, a demand, and an expectation to accomplish the goal listed. As you will see, there are many different ways to reach the same goal. Sometimes a rule is the best way to solve the problem, while in other cases a demand or an expectation may be more effective.

Goal	Using a Rule	Using a Demand	Using an Expectation
Getting the child to come home on time.			
Getting children to do their chores on time.			
Getting children to get along with each other.			
Keeping young children from running or playing in the street.			
Encouraging children to develop athletic, musical or academic talents.			

Principle 17

An organized home has work and play.

In my home we all had our own small chores to do. If we didn't do them we had to suffer the consequences which usually meant being grounded. Through these chores I learned that responsibility was part of having a job. When I found my first job outside the home, I already knew what responsibility was, and being responsible, I managed to get promotions over people who had been there longer than I. This helped my self-esteem very much and made me want to work that much harder. My parents taught me the importance of work, and how to enjoy work no matter what kind it may be.

Contrast the previous statement with this one

I compare myself to my girlfriend who never had Saturday chores. When we were little, I was so envious. Now I see how differently we've grown up. She never finished high school, had a baby out of wedlock, spent time in jail for drugs, and spent most of her adult life on welfare. She's told me since that she wished she would have had parents who cared enough to teach her to work so she would have learned to make something out of her life. I'm grateful that my parents cared enough to teach me to be productive.

Idea No. 1: An important part of teaching a child to be a responsible adult is to teach him how to work.

These two examples illustrate the significance of work and responsibility in even a young child's life. One very competent psychologist, when reviewing studies on moral development of children, concluded that one of the most effective ways to engender moral maturity is to assign work and responsibility to children.

I have previously suggested. . . that an important influence on a child learning to behave pro-socially is the focusing of responsibility on them by parents and other socializing agents to engage in behavior that enhances other's welfare.

Responsibility assignment may also be more structure; a child may be expected to take care of a younger sibling whenever the mother is not home or when she is otherwise occupied, or may have obligations for the maintenance and welfare of the family or some of its members.

I am proposing that involvement with responsible activities will lead to a sense of personal responsibility toward others, which, as the research has shown is an important influence on pro-social behavior.[42]

Work and responsibility seem to transform one's outlook of the world. It is as if a person must himself experience the fact that life does not simply meet his own personal needs; he must look beyond himself to understand the meaning of his existence. The importance of work has been stressed by those who have studied it. David Macarou, [43] for example, points out that some believe work to be a human instinct.

Idea No. 2: Work (including work for children) has historically been important both as a means and as an end in itself.

While it is believed that work develops a sense of responsibility, it is also true that man has assigned different meanings to work. In ancient Greece, work was at one time considered menial activity; for early Christians, it was God's punishment to mankind. It was the Protestant work ethic that eventually classified work as an end in itself, an ethical duty to be engaged in, not for material necessity, but because of resulting personal development.

The idea of hard work has also been abused, especially during the Industrial Revolution when young children were victimized by working long hours in deplorable conditions. Such abuses often affected physical and intellectual development for the worse.

However, this does not mean that work is necessarily undesirable for children. Often it is work conditions themselves and the purpose for work that must be considered. For example:

When I was a child living on a ranch in eastern Oregon, I had many opportunities to contribute to our family. We didn't have power lines where we lived, so we were without electricity. We used a wood-burning stove to cook our food and heat our home. The entire family worked together to get the wood we needed. We would go into the forest and Dad would cut a tree and saw it into blocks. Mom split the blocks with a maul and wedge, and my brothers and sister and I loaded it into the truck. At home we unloaded it, stacked it, and later carried it to the house. We all felt our contribution to be meaningful.

We also helped with the haying from a very early age. Dad would mow the hay, and he and Mom would rake it. Then he would load it onto a hay wagon and we would tramp it down so the wagon could carry a bigger load. We also helped tramp the hay into good, solid stacks once it was taken out of the field.

Some parents feel that in our modern, technologically advanced culture, it is impossible to provide this type of experience for children, but home management experts point out that there is ample work in the contemporary family. One successful way of organizing work in the family was related as follows:

In our family we were all expected to do chores. We sat down as a family and decided what was to be done, how it would be divided, and what the consequences would be if the work wasn't completed. We all had a voice in the matter, and all of us had to agree on the terms. It helped us in our work and chores to know *we all* had decided it.

Idea No. 3: Work with the family may be enjoyable as well as necessary.

A student related that one of the most enjoyable, pleasant childhood memories she had was working with her father each Saturday. Sometimes it was in the yard, sometimes in the basement, and sometimes it was doing errands around town. She loved to go with him and share his company. It made her feel important.

Idea No. 4: Work helps children learn to appreciate and care for their possessions.

Another benefit of work is the appreciation about life and hard-earned possessions that develops. The following story was related about a brother who came to value something he had worked for:

When my little brother was eight years old he wanted a certain skateboard very badly. The only problem was that the skateboard cost over $100. Mother told him that if he really wanted it, to save his money, and that he could also earn extra money by doing odd jobs around the house. She made sure there were plenty of things to be done and opportunities for him to earn that money. After a few months of long, hard work, he finally had enough money. That skateboard was his most prized possession and he guarded it with his life.

Idea No. 5: Work helps children be happier, get along with each other, learn new skills, and avoid boredom.

Perhaps the most significant attribute of work is its effect on children. When work (appropriate to the mental and physical abilities of the children) is diligently undertaken, better feelings abound and children are generally happier. One father noted that in his large family there frequently came times when children would say, "I don't know what to do." They would whine, fight, and become grouchy and negative. At such times he knew some type of activity was needed. Generally, he organized the home so that a short work assignment was given to each child and a small treat arranged at the task's completion.

He reports that almost without exception, this procedure resulted in greater happiness despite occasional reluctance by the children to participate.

A mother of ten reported the following:

After a few weeks of summer vacation I usually found that my children were tired of doing nothing. They were getting up late, complaining about boredom, fighting with each other and starting to make demands on my time and pocketbook. I have found that the solution to the boredom is to organize work projects and educational projects such as painting a room, cleaning out the garage, canning, making jam, sewing, etc. This usually ends the boredom and the fighting.

Idea No. 6: A child's play is his work.

Play is an activity that is equally important to a child's psychological and social development. Children have always played. In the ruins of ancient China, Egypt, and other ancient civilizations, toys have been found. Although once thought of as frivolous, even sinful and a waste of time, psychologists consider children's play as important, even critical for social and personality development. One psychologist stated, "play is the principal business of childhood.57 In a popular textbook on child psychology, Zanden [44] states the following about play:

1. It is a vehicle for cognitive stimulation.

2. It prepares children for life where they can experience themselves as active agents.

3. It provides opportunities for rehearsing adult roles.

4. It helps children build their own individual sense of identity.

5. It allows for both reality and fantasy; it is a medium that enables children to come to terms with their fears of villains, witches, ghosts, lions, dogs, and so on.

In almost every child psychology book, play is regarded as an important childhood activity. It is advisable to give children opportunity, time, toys, and encouragement in this activity. In one textbook picture a little girl is seated on the stairs with a dog, rabbit, mouse, jack-in-the-box, picture book, Raggedy Ann doll, and a baby bottle of milk at her feet.

Now move on to complete Learning Experiences 17.1 and 17.2.

LEARNING EXPERIENCE 17.1

Helping Children with Work and Play

Fill in the blanks in the following statements by choosing from the words listed at the bottom of the page.

1. Wise parents help children learn that work is _____ and _____ .

2. Work can be one of the most effective ways to engender _____ maturity.

3. Work can help a child develop _____ behavior.

4. Historical meanings of work have considered it to be _____, _____, _____ and an _____ .

5. Now work is less necessary economically, but it can be the source of pleasant childhood _____ .

6. Work also helps the child value _____ and _____ .

7. Work not only helps children develop responsibility and talents but also helps them avoid _____

8. Play is the principal _____ of childhood.

Word Choices:

Necessary	responsibility	Boredom	possession	Money	memories
Business	Pro-social	Ethical duty	Punishment	menial	enjoyable
important	Moral				

LEARNING EXPERIENCE 17.2

Self-Evaluation on Beliefs/Attitudes about Children's Work

Instructions: Circle Y for yes and N for no.

1. Y N   I had chores as a child.

2. Y N   I was envious of my friends who did not have to do chores.

3. Y N   I now believe that one of the most effective ways to engender moral maturity is to assign work and responsibility to children.

4. Y N   Involvement of children in responsible activities will lead to a sense of personal responsibility toward others—an important influence on pro-social behavior.

5. Y N   Parents should avoid abusing the idea of hard work for children as was done by some who made young children of the past work long hours in deplorable conditions.

6. Y N   Household work is particularly desirable because it is done together with other family members.

7. Y N   Saturday group work in the yard with father may be a particularly enjoyable activity for families.

8. Y N   Appreciation of material possessions is on a product of work responsibilities for children.

9. Y N   Children who work together find greater family closeness in spite of bickering among themselves.

10. Y N   Very young children learn about the world of work through their play.

11. Y N   When children in a large family do not have chores or work they end up fighting more.

Principle 18

An organized home has knowledge and truth.

A five-year-old was playing in the water when he hit his head and began to drown. Coughing and spitting, he was pulled out of the pool. As you might expect, he had a hard time getting back in the water. To help him overcome his fear, his parents enrolled him in a swimming class. Still, he resisted instructors who had a hard time even getting him to put his face in the water or to let go of the side of the pool. He had to repeat the class more than once. While driving home one day, the little boy began asking his father questions about death and dying. The next week he put his head under the water and swam. After this lesson the little boy said, "I swam today and I didn't die."

Idea No. 1: Children have a natural desire for knowledge and truth

Beliefs make a difference. The basis of personal confidence is knowledge and truth. When one does not understand his or her environment, the results of his or her actions, or the logic behind them, confidence gives way to uncertainty. For this reason, we seek to educate ourselves, to be informed, and to acquire knowledge. Man is curious and desires to know things. Even repressive governments have learned that they cannot keep man from seeking knowledge and truth, and we propose that a continuous input of knowledge and environmental stimuli is essential to healthy functioning. It is when the environment is devoid of content and stimuli that the child suffers and development is impaired.

Idea No. 2: If the child's environment is devoid of content and stimuli (learning), development is impaired.

Researchers have shown that when a person does not receive sensory stimulation, the mind begins to function erratically. [45] In one of his most dramatic experiments, Hebb paid subjects to do nothing for 24 hours a day.

They were placed on a comfortable bed and fed upon request, while wearing frosted-glass goggles that admitted light but allowed no vision. Their ears were covered with sponge rubber pillows to screen out noise.

They also wore gloves and, as much as possible, stimuli to the body was restricted. The results of this sensory deprivation were dramatic. Under these conditions, subjects showed significant loss in problem-solving skills, could not concentrate, were bored, were unable to sustain effort, scored lower on I.Q. tests, lost visual and motor coordination, and even began to hallucinate. While a child who is not learning does not experience such dramatic effects, an intellectual deprivation of sorts can retard future abilities.

Idea No. 3: The ideal environment for a child includes both knowledge and truth.

The ideal climate for children is one in which both information and truth are amply available. Not only should children's questions be answered, but truth is important. This is not to say that children cannot believe in Santa Claus but if they can find honest answers to their questions they will develop more. Parents should consider the readiness of the child and not try to give answers beyond the comprehension of the child. Also, although parents need not know everything, they should try to answer questions and find the answers and truthfully tell the child when he does not know the answer.

Idea No. 4: For children as well as adults, knowledge is power.

An attitude of respect for truth and knowledge is important. For example, the father in the following account helped his daughter learn the importance of intelligent problem solving.

I wanted a hamster. I knew that my mother didn't like rodents, but that she would go along with my father if he said it was alright. I also knew that my usual methods of convincing my father in situations like this didn't work very well. So I had to change. A short time ago I had been the unwilling recipient of one of my father's lectures about the virtues of information and knowledge. I thought, why not try it, it can't hurt. So I went to the library and read all kinds of material on hamsters, their habits, characteristics, and care and feeding. Then I sat down and figured out all the reasons why I should have a hamster, all the reasons against it, and counter-arguments to what I expected my father to say. It worked so well I was absolutely amazed. Armed with all my information, I went in to talk with him. Fifteen minutes later we were on our way to the pet store to buy a hamster. That one experience made more of an impression on me than all the lectures my father had ever given about the value of knowledge.

Idea No. 5: The child depends heavily on parents for accurate information.

Sometimes it is hard for a parent to provide knowledge or to be honest with a child. It may seem at the moment that it would be more kind to allow an error to pass unnoticed. But the child depends heavily on parents for accurate information. Consider the following episode:

A child had been working on spelling new words and had finally mastered a difficult word. He went proudly to his mother and spelled the word to her. In the process he missed one letter. The mother did not correct the child. The child then went to his father to spell the word for him. Several months later the child quizzically asked the mother why she had not corrected him.

In our parenting class, we often debate whether it was fair and wise for the following mother to share with her children the upsetting and personal circumstances behind her separation from their father:

A year ago, my father left my family, which was a total shock and surprise. My mother, needing support and wanting to do the right thing, felt it better to inform my sister and I about the circumstances involved in the separation and the reasons behind it. She thought we were old enough and mature enough to handle it.

When discussed in class, most students felt that even though it might produce mental stress and anguish for young children, it is better for them to understand personal things such as divorce, death, adult mistakes, and family finances. However, parents should not dump all their heavy emotional problems on children. This logic underlies the consensus among professionals that parents should talk about sex education with their children. It is understood that the type and amount of information given should be appropriate to the child's maturity level and ability to comprehend.

Idea No. 6: Experience is often the most effective teacher of knowledge and truth.

While the emphasis has thus far been on placing knowledge and truth at the child's disposal when he or she is ready to receive it, it is sometimes necessary to arrange learning experiences that are designed to increase understanding. A visit to the zoo, educational films, trips, visiting sick relatives in the hospital, and other planned experiences provide enrichment. For example, instead of preaching about the dangers of playing with matches, a student said his mother did the following:

Mother had problems with my two oldest brothers, Tony and Mike, when they were kids. They liked to play with matches. Mom told them not to, but they would hide and play with them anyway. Mom was really worried that they would hurt themselves or someone else. So she sat them down in a safe place and let them play with as many matches as they wanted to. After they burned their fingers a few times while sitting there, they decided playing with matches wasn't as much fun as they had previously thought.

Experience in handling hazardous parts of our environment can often increase competence and decrease personal danger. Like the previous example, this can apply to firearms, knives, animals, and automobiles.

Idea No. 7: At first a positive self-concept may be more helpful than an accurate one.

The need for truth and knowledge about the outside, physical environment has been emphasized. An understanding of the environment engenders social competence. Also important is that which we learn about ourselves from the knowledge and truth available to us. In many discussions on the self, it is simply pointed out that one should have a positive self-concept. The need for an accurate and realistic understanding of the self is often overlooked. In reviewing research on the self-concept, a distinguished child psychologist, Boyd McCandless [46] states:

This study summarized immediately above suggested honesty about oneself, which may also be thought of as accuracy, as an important aspect in the self-concept and may be related to good adjustment. Two studies then, suggest clearly that accuracy of self-estimate is associated with a number of other indices of good adjustment. Although another study suggests that this relationship is affected by whether the self-concept is *high and accurate* or *low and accurate*, the former condition would be more likely to accompany good adjustment.

It is difficult to know whether it is more important to have a positive self-concept or an accurate self-concept. Ideally, the optimal self-concept would be both accurate and positive. Imagine you have two mirrors to look into each morning before you leave to face the world. One mirror is in a well-lighted room. It reflects you accurately, showing all blemishes and imperfections. Looking into this mirror is sometimes discouraging as you are likely to note each of your imperfections. The other mirror, one away from adequate light, tends to reflect a more pleasing image. After looking at yourself in this mirror, you generally conclude that you look pretty sharp. It is a question of which mirror best prepares you for the day ahead. For young children it is important that they have a positive mirror as they start each day. We recommend beginning by developing a positive self-concept and then emphasizing accuracy.

As you conclude thinking about this principle, remember that even if you agree with it, the real task is to apply it to the lives of your children. Many examples have been given to help you begin to understand how to accomplish this task. Learning Experience 18.1 is designed to help you remember specific points that have been presented.

LEARNING EXPERIENCE 18.1

Self-Test on Children's Need for Knowledge and Truth

Circle the correct response.

1. T F A child has a natural desire for knowledge and truth.

2. T F A child's development is impaired if his environment lacks of content and stimulation for learning.

3. T F A child needs truthful answers to many questions.

4. T F "Knowledge is power" works for children as well as adults.

5. T F Often it is better to give a child accurate information rather than purposely overlook mistakes.

6. T F Children often prefer to have honest, accurate information, even though the truth may be painful to them.

7. T F Parents should avoid dumping heavy emotional problems on their children.

8. T F The type and amount of information given to children should be appropriate to the child's maturity level and ability to comprehend.

9. T F Parents should arrange learning experiences appropriate to the ages and needs of the children.

10. T F Accurate knowledge about the self is conducive to good adjustment.

11. T F The ideal self-concept would be both accurate and positive.

Idea No. 4: For children as well as adults, knowledge is power.

Idea No. 5: The child depends heavily on parents for accurate information.

Idea No. 6: Experience is often the most effective teacher of knowledge and truth.

Idea No. 7: An accurate self-concept is important, but a positive one may be more useful at first.

Principle 19

An organized home has values and beliefs.

I felt that something had broken within me and on which my life had always rested, that I had nothing left to hold on to, and that morally my life had stopped. . . .

Behold me then, a man happy and in good health, hiding the rope in order not to hang myself to the rafters of the room where every night I went to sleep alone; behold me no longer going shooting, lest I should yield to the too easy temptation of putting an end to myself with my gun.

All this took place when so far as all my outer circumstances went, I ought to have been completely happy. I had a good wife who loved me and whom I loved; good children and a large property which was increasing with no pains on my part. I was more respected by my kinsfolk and acquaintances than I had ever been; I was with praise by strangers; and without exaggeration I could believe my name already famous. Moreover I was neither insane nor ill. On the contrary, I possessed a physical and mental strength which I have rarely met in persons of my age. I could mow as well as the peasant, I could work with my brain eight hours uninterruptedly and feel no bad effects. . . .

What will be the outcome of what I do today? Of what I shall do tomorrow? What will be the outcome of all my life? Why should I live? Why should I do anything? Is there in life any purpose which the inevitable death which awaits me does not undo and destroy?

These questions are the simplest in the world. From the stupid child to the wisest old man, they are in the soul of every human being. Without an answer to them, it is impossible... [47]

Idea No. 1: The foundation for understanding life and its purpose and meaning begins in childhood.

While the famous author, Leo Tolstoy, [47] wrote this about himself as an adult, the foundation for understanding life, its purpose and meaning, begins during childhood. The purposes of one's life need to be sought, although indoctrination into a specific religion or ideology is not the object.

One of the most respected and popular textbook writers on personal adjustment speaks of our need to solve human problems:

[He speaks of] our need to solve the uniquely human problems of acquiring both "know-how" and "know-why." For the individual, this means trying to find the answers to three key questions: Who am I? Where am I going? [48]

Idea No. 2: Children need a value system that gives meaning to life.

A survey of personal adjustment books reveals the belief that men must find meaning in their lives for optimal functioning. Writing about the creative life, Clark Moustakas popular theortican and author [49] states:

Morality is relevant to healthy existence. Without this ethical and value dimension, such gains in personality as release of tension, freedom in self-disclosure, and self-insight are destitute of enduring value. Moral geniuses are not required--but people are needed who are morally alive and able to communicate directly with their fellow beings.

Practicing therapists repeatedly stress the importance of meaning in one's life. What does this mean to parents? Essentially, parents can help children consider their existence and present them with a rational value system. Traditionally, this has been done through various belief systems, religions, values, and attitudes.

The value system presented to the child need not be formal but it must be salient. This means that parents must speak about right and wrong, and purpose and meaning. It is best to do this in a spirit of freedom and choice rather than imposing absolutes upon the child.

Idea No. 3: Example is often the best teacher of moral values.

Example and style of living are perhaps the two most practical ways to bring meaning into existence. One student describes her family as follows:

While living at home, I never saw my parents lie, steal, or put something over on someone. They were honest with everyone and as I grew older, I realized that their values prevented a lot of day-to-day problems and worries. Also, my parents would punish us worse if we lied than if we just took the blame for a particular wrong-doing. That provided an incentive to tell the truth.

Consider another illustration:

The best example of service I have ever witnessed is my mother. People always call her when something needs to be done because they know that she is helpful and dependable. Also commendable, I feel, is what she does to make others happy. About once a week she makes a special cake or fresh bread, or something else homemade and has it anonymously delivered to a family. She wants them to know that they are special.

It would appear obvious that these mothers effectively modeled and probably instilled certain values in the lives of their children.

Idea No. 4: Some children rebel against the values both taught and modeled by parents and then later return to those values.

Whether parents quietly portray their values or exhort, preach, and insist that a set of values be accepted, some children will rebel. One student writes:

After all this teaching and structuring of our values and beliefs, one of my brothers rebelled and escaped to live in another value system, which of course had different beliefs. His wasn't a forceful, violent rebellion, but rather an outward demonstration that he had his own beliefs and values and would no longer follow the rest of the family.

Fortunately, in this particular instance the parents allowed him freedom and he eventually came back and accepted the values he had seen modeled by his parents and other family members.

A dramatic example of how meaning is demonstrated to be important for psychological functioning is given by Victor Frankl, a psychotherapist. At the age of 37, Frankl was subjected to a three-year ordeal of torture and cruelty in the Auschwitz concentration camp. He was one of few to survive this ordeal and attributes his endurance to a belief in the human capacity to find meaning and purpose in life in the face of overwhelming suffering. Gordon Allport wrote the following in the preface of Frankl's book, *Man's Search for Meaning:*

How could he—every possession lost, every value destroyed, suffering from hunger, cold, brutality, hourly expecting extermination—how could he find life preserving? A psychiatrist who personally has faced such extremity is a psychiatrist worth listening to. [50]

Idea No. 5: Three factors important to obtaining a vital sense of meaning and purpose in life are: (1) spirituality; (2) freedom; and responsibility.

Frankl's theory stresses the important of possessing a "will to meaning." His psychological theory is called logotherapy, which is translated from the Greek word "logos" or "meaning." For Frankl, a lack of meaning in life creates neurosis. In one form it is characterized by meaninglessness, purposelessness, aimlessness, and emptiness in life. He had seen this not only in the lives of his fellow prisoners at Auschwitz, but also in his patients. To overcome this neurosis Frankl proposes that a person must obtain a vital sense of meaning and purpose in life. Three factors are necessary to facilitate this process: spirituality, freedom, and responsibility.

While Frankl's logotherapy is treatment-oriented, his principles can be applied toward creating a preventive environment. In this case, the parent, by providing meaning for a child, develops a climate for healthy personality development.

Principle 20

An organized home meets physical needs and is safe.

Between the sixth and seventh grades, my family moved to a large city. Two girls at the start of that seventh year decided it would be fun to pick on me. I was harassed by these two girls for two years. They never left me alone—going to school, at school, or coming from school. They used physical as well as verbal abuse, and I was so averse to fighting that I just took it all. I was so fearful that my grades hit rock bottom! I would cry at night because I had made it home safely. In any case, because I was in such fear for my safety I could not function properly.

Idea No. 1: People need fulfillment of basic physical needs for food and safety before they can be productively involved in other pursuits.

The removal of security in this young girl's life had a tremendous impact on her daily routine. Imagine the possible devastation had she not had a secure home. Under constant fear, it would have been impossible to function properly in other areas of her life.

Similarly, deprivation of physical needs is also disrupting and can produce lasting effects. One student writes about her father:

My father's parents died while he was quite young and he was therefore raised by his older brothers and sisters (the oldest being 16 at the time of their parents' death). He went without many physical necessities. They didn't always have enough to eat and their housing was poor. My father has expressed to me many times the lack of security that he felt because he didn't know from one day to the next if he would get enough to eat or if he would have proper clothes to wear. He worried about these conditions so much that he would become lax in his school work or get behind because he had to go out and earn money. It would appear that people need to take care of their physical needs before they can become productively involved in other pursuits. He has seen to it that we have all of our physical needs met. Even now, after I have been in college for five years, he always asks if I have enough to eat, if I am sleeping right, and if the house is warm enough.

These two examples illustrate a fundamental psychological concept proposed by Abraham Maslow in 1943: a theory of human motivation that even today continues to have appeal. He stated that people begin their lives by satisfying basic needs and then moving to higher needs. Before a person can meet higher needs, lower needs must have been adequately satisfied. He said it this way:

If all needs aren't satisfied and the organism is then dominated by the physical needs, all other needs become simply nonexistent or are pushed into the background. . . . For the man who is extremely and dangerously hungry, no other interest exists. He dreams food, he remembers food, he thinks about food, . . . and he wants only food. . . life itself tends to be defined in terms of eating. Anything else will be defined as unimportant. Freedom, love, community feeling, respect, and philosophy may all be waved aside as fripperies which are useless since they fail to fill the stomach. Such a man may fairly be said to live by bread alone. [51]

Maslow has qualified his theory to explain how some people become independent and rise above physical and safety needs. But what is important here is the obvious and supportable belief that a healthy, positive growth climate needs to provide safety, health care, and physical necessities to ensure the proper development of psychological and social needs.

Idea No. 2: A child needs safety—not only protection from physical danger but also the safety of a predictable, orderly, and consistent home environment.

Maslow's proposed safety needs include more general elements than those of actual physical and emotional threats. Maslow states:

Another indication of the child's need for safety is his preference for orderliness, for a kind of undisturbed routine or rhythm period. He seems to want a predictable, orderly world. For instance, injustice, unfairness, or inconsistency in the parents seems to make a child feel anxious and unsafe. This may not be so much because of the injustice *per se* or any particular pains involved, but rather because of the fact that this threatens to make the world look unreliable or unsafe or unpredictable. Perhaps one could express this more succinctly by saying that the child needs an organized world rather than an unorganized, unstructured one. [52]

Obviously, a safe, nourishing, physical climate is more complicated than would appear at first glance. We will now look more specifically at aspects of the physical environment that have been shown to have powerful impact on psychological development.

Idea No. 3: Physical deprivations such as those involving sleep and food result in psychological and personality problems.

Physical needs include food, water, air, sleep, and shelter. Without question, deprivation of these would have serious physiological effects, but would deprivation also adversely influence psychological development?

The effects of inadequate or improper physical needs may not be direct, and therefore, specific influences upon children have not yet been demonstrated. However, studies exist that show air pollution to have negative effects on physiological functioning. Similarly, failure to provide conditions conducive to sleep has negative psychological effects. Sleep deprivation in adults leads to behavior that is similar to that of drunkenness: incoherence, rambling speech, decreased coordination, and even hallucinations. [53] To generalize from sleep-deprivation research on adults to children is not methodologically sound, but it seems reasonable to suppose that when children are not allowed adequate sleep, changes in consciousness and coordination might have undesirable effects on psychological development.

Chronically malnourished children experience growth retardation not only physically, but also psychologically. Tests show a decline in mental abilities with prolonged food-deprivation. [54] Malnutrition directly affects psychological development by impairing neurological growth due to a non-availability of amino acids for protein concentration in brain tissue. However, indirect effects are seen in altered motivational states, and decreased energy and strength. These secondary effects were illustrated in an experiment by Shineor. [55] In this study, conscientious objectors to military service volunteered to be deprived of food for a number of weeks. They became irritable, obsessed by thoughts of food, discouraged, had periods of depression, and were unable to sustain mental and physical effort.

Idea No. 4: Physical deprivations of a child's basic needs may be unrelated to financial difficulties.

That adults should provide for the safety and physical needs of children seems obvious, yet many adults fail to provide. Failure to meet physical needs does not simply result in temporary discomfort but impedes necessary psychological development. Physical neglect may manifest itself indirectly through a neglected child's appearance. A dirty face, ragged clothes, and a runny nose do not elicit from others the kind of attention, caring, and affection that we hope would be shown a young child. In addition, a lack of motivation or attention resulting from poor nutrition is interpreted as laziness, stupidity, or indifference, thus eliciting negative and hostile responses from others.

Parents experiencing financial difficulties can, nonetheless, ensure that their children's clothes are attractive; that their children are washed and neatly groomed; and that they have balanced, though often simple meals. Adequate food and clothing need not be expensive; healthy food may be grown and used clothing may be obtained at little or no cost with time and effort. The disadvantages of a limited budget can be overcome.

Physical deprivation may also happen when there is plenty of money but little time available to care for the physical needs of the child. Children left to "self care" may eat expensive junk food with little or no nutritional value. They may wear expensive or stylish clothing that is inappropriate, offensive, or unclean.

Idea No. 5: Parents sometimes wisely shield their children from fears concerning family finances.

Sometimes environmental deficiency is more imagined than real. If a child is insecure and frightened because he feels he doesn't have "good" clothes and food like his friends, it does not matter that a parent may have concluded that there is no threat to his safety or welfare. In such cases, the child's imagined interpretation is as real as if a physical threat actually existed. The child's fears should be acknowledged and attempts made to alleviate these fears. In some instances, it may be wise for the parent to conceal real environmental difficulties. In one family, the parents did this in an ingenious way:

This family had an "emergency bank." Whenever the family ran into financial problems, the parents would tell the children that they could use money from the bank, but they would rather make it without bothering the money in their "emergency bank" if they could. So, all the children did whatever they could to earn money, and they never did have to use the "emergency bank" funds. Years later, the children found out that there was no "emergency bank," but because they had all along believed otherwise, they never grew up with a fear that often accompanies poverty. times.

You are likely to find the information presented here rather straightforward and easy to understand. Learning Experience 20.1 is to help you determine the extent to which you see this principle as important.

LEARNING EXPERIENCE 20.1

Meeting Physical Needs and Making Home Safe

Circle the number of the answer that best fits your feelings about each of the statements below. (**ANSWER KEY: 1=Never Agree; 2=Sometimes Agree; 3=Usually Agree; 4=Always Agree**)

1. 1 2 3 4   When a person is in fear for his safety he cannot function properly socially or otherwise.

2. 1 2 3 4   People must take care of their physical needs before they can become productively involved in other pursuits.

3. 1 2 3 4   People begin their lives by satisfying basic needs and then moving to higher needs.

4. 1 2 3 4   The person who is deprived of food can think of little else.

5. 1 2 3 4   Children have a need for an organized world with regular routines.

6. 1 2 3 4   Deprivation of a person's need for sleep has negative psychological effects

7. 1 2 3 4   Food deprivation in children results in impaired mental and psychological growth.

8. 1 2 3 4   Even if finances are limited, parents can provide adequate clothing and nutrition for their children.

9. 1 2 3 4   Children in homes with plenty of money but left to "self-care" may also suffer physical deprivation.

10. 1 2 3 4   The financial fears of children are real and should be acknowledged by parents.

11. 1 2 3 4   Children should be appropriately shielded from most financial stress.

SUMMARY

Instructions: Mark *a* if the statement is true and *b* of it is false.

1. High expectations generally produce timid and inhibited children.

2. Expectations have three basic elements.

3. An expectation is the same as a rule or a demand.

4. Although work with the family is not enjoyable, it is necessary.

5. Play is the principle work of childhood.

6. If a child's environment is lacking knowledge, truth, content, or learning stimuli, their development will be impaired.

7. Fortunately, children do not have to depend on parents for accurate information in the modern world, with the aid of schools, churches, television and libraries.

8. The type and amount of information given to children should be appropriate to the child's maturity level and ability to comprehend.

9. The foundation for understanding life and its purposes begins in adolescence.

10. The factors most important in obtaining a sense and meaning of purpose are freedom and responsibility.

LESSON FIVE

The Advantages of Being Positive

After you have successfully completed this lesson, you should be able to do the following:

1. Explain why a positive approach to parenting is more effective.

2. Discuss the effects of punishment and reward.

3. Recognize how to use encouragement in developing desired behaviors.

Principle 21

Encourage good behavior with rewards.

Whenever we asked Byron to do something that he didn't want to do, he whined, threw himself on the floor, and moaned "Aw-w-w" or complained, "Oh, brother," or yelled, "That's not fair. Why do I always have to do it?" He would also stomp his feet, throw his arms down, or just plain cry.

As I thought over how we could change his behavior, I realized we should first look at our behavior as parents. I sensed that we were in a slump of being a little negative toward our children. We have sometimes been too hard on them if they weren't doing things just right. And so I decided that the first step in changing Byron's behavior was to become more positive with him.

Idea No. 1: The most documented principle in psychology is "rewards work."

We will continue with this mother's statement about how she successfully applied the reward system with her own modifications. She used the most solidly-documented principle in psychology which is: "Rewards Work!" [56]

Idea No. 2: Talking with children about problem behaviors can gain their cooperation.

Then the next thing I did was to explain to Byron what he was doing and how it made me feel. We talked over some of the responses he had been making, and I asked him how he would like it if I were to answer him that way. He answered, "Not very well."

For the next step I decided to ignore his inappropriate behavior and praise him for responding in the desired way. I let him know how good it made me feel, and the special feeling that came into our family when he answered the desirable way. I was very specific about the behavior I wanted to reinforce and included a lot of hugs and loving.

This new behavior of expressing himself without whining, etc., has become part of how Byron wants to act. He has said, "I like talking without whining," and "I'm glad I don't do that anymore."

Idea No. 3: Rewarding desired behavior helps children change.

Actions which are followed by positive consequences become stronger. This simple principle has been tested and advocated in business management, medicine, schools, and literally every segment of our complex society. Experts and consultants dress up this same principle with fancy names, but the underlying message is the same: "Behaviors which are rewarded become stronger." Now, where does this principle fit in with parenting?

Recently, the most popular child-rearing experts have been telling stories of spoiled children terrorizing their parents. They report children who are out of control--lacking respect and self-control. Shocked parents are asking, "What can be done?" The latest answer is "Get tough." Often the recommended way to "get tough" is to use more control and punishment which, in many cases, may be needed temporarily because parents have given up their leadership role.

We realize parents should take charge and assume leadership, but generally a positive emphasis is preferred. In the long run, a positive approach will result in more long-lasting change and more effective parental leadership.

What is the reward system? Fortunately, this principle is straightforward: arrange life events so that positive behaviors are followed by rewards.

Idea No. 4: Using the reward system requires three simple steps.

From a family leadership point of view, the reward principle is put into action following these steps:

Develop or obtain as many positive rewards as possible. Put these at your disposal. First, there are materials things such as money and food. Then there are activities such as group trips or movies. Third, there are social-emotional experiences such as attention, recognition, or honors.

Decide in advance what your general long-term behavioral objectives are. Then for your children, specify these in simple, easy to attain, small steps.

Plentifully give rewards as these steps are progressively accomplished. As success is achieved, you will not have to reward as frequently.

Idea No. 5: Plan ahead both long-term behavioral objectives as well as rewards for desired behavior.

An objection is sometimes raised that you are bribing or manipulating children. The answer is that the whole world is organized according to this principle: successful behavior is rewarded. Simply because rewards are organized by a parent is not sufficient reason to object to a successful program. We have provided a checklist to help determine if the reward system you have planned is effective.

1. Do I have rewards that mean a lot to my child?

2. Can I clearly state just what behaviors I expect?

3. Do I start with small enough steps to make it easy for my child to meet my expectations?

4. Am I in control of my own emotions so I can present my rewards with control and patience?

5. Do I teach with action and avoid too much talking?

6. Am I willing to follow through even when other important demands are placed upon me?

You can't use the reward system unless you have rewards. To help you realize how many rewards you have as a parent, study Table 21.1. Most parents have encountered the principle of rewarding behavior in everyday life. It should require only a little focus on some key principles to help you become an expert in using rewards to increase positive behavior in your parenting.

The key to successful implementation of the reward system is to use the rewards at your disposal. Leadership failures often occur because parents are unaware of the power which is at their disposal. The error too often made is to give all privileges to the children and then when the children misbehave, try to take them back again. It is better to first expect good behavior and then reward.

Anger is elicited when something is given and taken back. However, if the rewards were not given away in the first place, there is surprisingly little or no resentment in their absence. For example, in a family where the free use of the car has been given, there is resentment when the father, in retaliation for unacceptable behavior, tells his son he cannot use the car this weekend. The syndrome of the unappreciated adolescent occurs most when the adolescent assumes he has a free ride in his life. Appreciation occurs when those resources which have been obtained and earned by the parent are generously given as a parent's way of saying, "Thanks for your responsible behavior." Now the parent could add, "Also, you can use the car Friday night."

Idea No. 6: Rewards work: your success depends on implementation and the choice of goals you are trying to reach.

Table 21.1 is a list of parental powers. They are divided into the following categories: home, personal help activities, outside home help, possessions, activities, social-emotional. We feel social and emotional consequences should not be taken away but given in greater abundance as a special consequence. Activities and social-emotional rewards are probably the best overall rewards. To learn how to best use rewards, first study the list of resources and powers in Table 21.1

TABLE 21.1

Parental Resources and Powers

Check which of the following you can or do use as positive consequences for good behavior and/or negative consequences for undesirable behavior.

HOME	POSSESSIONS
Meals	Use of car
Use of TV	Use of computer
Use of musical equipment	Use of stereo and Video
Use of rooms	Use of Phones
Books	Discount tickets
Furniture	Games
Invitation for friends to visit	
Parties (birthday, sleep overs, etc.)	
Toys	
Clothing	

OUTSIDE THE HOME HELP

Transportation
Money
Flnding jobs
!Enrolling in recreational activities
!Enrolling in Lesson
Signing for auto purchase
Insurance
Trips
Help getting along siblings
Help getting along teachers
Help getting along peers

YOUR PERSONAL HELP

Help with homework
Help with cleaning
Transportation to activities
Answering questions

ACTIVITIES

Attendance at extracurricular
Activiities
Summer vacations
Free at 110me after school
Saturdays
Family games

SOCIAL EMOTIONS

Affection
Company of siblings
Attention
Time together
Compliments
Games and Sporting events
Visiting and conversation
Listening to prolblems of child
Helping solve problems of child

Principle 22

Most parents don't want to use punishment.

Possibly a parent's greatest concerns are to "train up the child in the way he should go" and to control a child's misbehavior. Unfortunately, some parents use punishment ineffectively. As you read the following story, the inappropriate use of power will be obvious.

We heard Dad coming home and we all ran away and hid. Some of us crawled under our beds and others climbed in closets and hid. My little sister had broken the guardrail to keep the babies from falling down the stairs and we all knew that Dad would be mad. He screamed his range, and everyone stayed quiet and hidden. Then he found one of my little sisters and he screamed at her and threatened to spank her hard unless she told him who did it or who was the oldest one at home. (Being the oldest one at home meant you were responsible for anything that happened.) I was the oldest one home that time and I could hear my sister screaming, "Daddy, I didn't do it. I didn't do it." She told him she didn't know who did it. She told him where I was and I got a spanking so hard that the marks lasted for weeks. Then he wanted me to tell him I loved him. I didn't love him. I hated him for being so mean and unfair.

It was so unfair. I hadn't broken the guardrail and it was just a little thing that could be fixed quickly.

Because he was angry and didn't want to have to fix anything.

Punishment comes all too naturally. "I'll teach him" or "She won't get away with that," are common expressions preceding punishment. It is so simple to inflict pain on someone else if they are not doing what you want. History tells us that the paddle, the whip, and even instruments for torture have been devised to stop others from deviating. Some parents while deploring physical punishment, find themselves engaging in social, emotional, or psychological punishment.

Idea No. 1: Punishment does have an immediate effect.

The origin of this tendency to punish one another is elusive, but the reason for punishment's continuance is simple. When we punish, something happens! Punishment does have an immediate effect. Even if it doesn't permanently stop undesirable behavior it disrupts the pattern. Some psychologists maintain that punishment simply suppresses behavior or causes the punished child to disguise his actions so he won't be detected. Even so, this temporary suppression or disguise seems to the parent—at least at the time—preferable to having the action blatantly continued. There is concrete evidence that physical punishment can weaken, eliminate, and/or suppress behavior but there is a price to be paid.[57]

Idea No. 2: Physical punishment often harms the parent-child relationship and thus limits the parent's ability to "train up the child in the way he should go."

Most parents do not really like to punish their children, especially if other more effective means of changing behavior are available. Physical punishment may only stop the behavior temporarily and therefore, is ineffective. Punitive measures like those in the examples, are too often administered in rage and then injure the parent-child relationship. Since the real key to controlling a child's behavior requires a positive parent-child relationship, you can readily see that this kind of physical punishment does not contribute to changing behavior permanently. Additionally, violent outbursts of anger expressed in painful physical punishment are counterproductive to the hopes and dreams of the happy home-life that most parents have for their children.

Idea No. 3: Punishment should match the misbehavior and should be understood by the child.

In an attempt to identify practical and humane procedures for using punishment for inappropriate behavior in children, one author recommended the following for parents to consider before using punishment:

Do not use physical punishment when emotionally upset.

Consider using nonphysical methods of punishment such as removing privileges or verbal punishment which are generally preferable.

Be sure to provide clear instructions as to what is an acceptable alternative when using punishment.

Avoid time lags between the time one threatens punishment and actually delivers the consequences.

Punishment should match the misbehavior; a behavior that has important consequences should be punished more severely than a behavior of less importance. A trivial matter is best not punished or punishment becomes trivial.

Tell the child precisely what he or she is being punished for. [58]

Idea No. 4: Sometimes punishment is both appropriate and necessary.

While many psychologists hesitate to advocate the use of punishment, there are some occasions when it seems appropriate. Two child psychologists write:

1. A mild punishment may be necessary to *teach a child what no means.* A young child learns the meaning of the word no or no-no by having the words spoken at the same instant that something unpleasant happens to him--for example, a loud, gruff voice or a slap on the hand.

2. In emergencies, punishment may be the only way to *save a person from greater danger.* A tetanus shot is punishment, but it is considered necessary to save a child from greater danger. Dental work may be punishment but is less painful in the long run than bad teeth or gums. Knocking a child to the ground is punishment, but if it removes him from the path of a line drive baseball or a rifle bullet, then the punishment is the lesser of the two evils.

3. Punishment may be the only way to *get a child to try some alternative behavior* which can then be reinforced. An undesirable pattern of behavior may be so well-established that the child would never try any alternative without some shake-up in his regular routine.

4. A young child may not understand reason, and the use of physical punishment may be the most effective and necessary means. An example is the two or three-year-old child who fails warnings to stay out of a street. street. [59]

Idea No. 5: Punishment may have negative consequences not intended by the punisher.

These same psychologists, however, also listed some clear dangers in using punishment:

A punishment may actually be reinforcing. A teacher who punishes a child by making him sit in front next to her desk or by writing his name on the blackboard calls attention to the child. The fact that other children notice him may actually be reinforcing, thereby increasing rather than reducing his undesirable behavior.

When a child receives frequent punishment and sees no course of action that will enable him to escape that punishment, a foundation is laid for later neurotic behavior.

Children tend to resist punishment by fighting back, actively escaping, or withdrawing into passive apathy. Vandalism, truancy, and uncooperativeness are names frequently given such forms of resistance when they occur in school. They are the direct result of the punishment adults mete out to children.

The child tends to avoid the punisher whenever he can. A child who has constantly been punished by his parents does not want to be near them any more than he has to be. In families where punishment is frequently used, grown children may feel uncomfortable around their parents. Children can develop severe feelings of guilt if they have been taught they should love their parents but in fact do not. When you love someone, you want to be near him; but you do not want to be near someone who punishes you. You cannot want to be near a person who punishes you without undergoing some kind of inner conflict. Parents and teachers who want their children to love them should maximize positive reinforcement opportunities and minimize the use of punishment.

Now turn to the Learning Experience on the next page to explore your own feelings about punishment. After doing that, nine substitutes for punishment will be presented.

LEARNING EXPERIENCE 22.1

Self-Test on Exploring Your Feelings about Punishment

For each of the statements below, circle the answer that best states your feelings about punishment. (**ANSWER KEY: SA=Strongly Agree; A=Agree; NS=Not Sure; D=Disagree; SD=Strongly Disagree**)

1. Physical punishment is effective and stops the behavior.

   SA   A   NS   D   SD

2. Parents should match punishment to the severity of the misbehavior.

   SA   A   NS   D   SD

3. Parents should not punish in anger.

   SA   A   NS   D   SD

4. Parents should be sure that children understand why they are being punished.

   SA   A   NS   D   SD

5. When children feel that the punishment is fair, they are more likely to learn from the experience.

   SA   A   NS   D   SD

6. Harsh physical punishment that is not understood or unfair interfere with the parent-child relationship and thereby limit parent effectiveness.

   SA   A   NS   D   SD

7. Sometimes, in an emergency, physical punishment may be beneficial and the best choice under the circumstances.

   SA   A   NS   D   SD

8. Sometimes punishment is necessary to get a child to try an alternative behavior.

   SA   A   NS   D   SD

9. A parent who punishes in rage and with no good reason may simply be abusive.

SA   A   NS   D   SD

In those cases where I have used (or think I would use) physical punishment, I found the following: **(Answer T=True or F=False)**

a. _____ I enjoyed punishing.

b. _____ It was frustrating.

c. _____ It took more time than expected to resolve conflict.

d. _____ It was highly-effective.

Principle 23

Behavior stops when it is not rewarded: goals of misbehavior.

In a special English class the boy frequently threw tantrums involving crying, kicking, and screaming. It was a common occurrence to see attendants drag the kicking and screaming boy out of class, attracting a large audience of staff members. Most onlookers believed the tantrums occurred when the boy was frustrated or teased. The teacher, however, noticed that the tantrums were not temporally associated with the child being teased or frustrated. Instead she saw the tremendous amount of attention given him at those times. She decided to eliminate the tantrum behavior through an extinction process.

The next time a tantrum occurred, a teacher asked the attendants to bring the boy to her room. The attendants placed the boy at her desk and left the room. The teacher closed the door and waited. She told the boy that when he had finished crying, they could start working. The boy cried for approximately eight minutes and then said he was ready to work. The teacher then went to her desk to help him with his English exercises, and the boy was cooperative for the remainder of the class period. [60]

What do you do when you don't want to physically punish or use guilt, fear, and shame to eliminate undesirable behavior? Parents know that some behaviors cannot be tolerated. They justifiably ask, "What can I do?" Several excellent alternatives are available.

Clearly, the simplest established way to eliminate negative behavior is to see that the behavior is not rewarded. In many cases it is surprising to notice the great variety of rewards actually following a behavior. Attention, for example, is given to many misbehaving children, and often that is exactly what they want.

Tommy is very frustrating. He seems to know when I need to be left alone. When I try to sew or mend clothing or work on the computer he pesters me to help him with something else. When I am talking on the telephone he creates an emergency or yells for me to help him. It's hard for me to get anything done.

Building on this belief that misbehavior is usually motivated by the desire for attention, a short outline of one psychologist's, Dreikurs, analysis will be presented. (61), (62), (63), (64)

Idea No. 1: The first goal of misbehavior is attention-getting.

The first goal of misbehavior, attention-getting, is usually very easy to identify. For example, if a parent sits down to write a letter, an attention-seeking child might start crawling on his lap. The child seems to assume he is important only when attended to. Yielding to these demands increases the child's belief that his assumption is true.

Idea No. 2: Attention-getting activities may be constructive or destructive.

Attention can be constructively or destructively gained. A child actively seeking attention through constructive channels is often viewed as a successful, yet somewhat obnoxious child. This child's only measuring stick for success is the amount of attention and praise he receives for a particular act. In other words, the activity is only successful when attention from a significant source (parent, teacher, etc.) accompanies the activity.

The child actively seeking attention through destructive channels is labeled a nuisance. He leaves messes, fights, and makes noise-- anything to keep the parent or teacher busy with him. As long as his destructive activities gain the goal of attention he will persist.

Idea No. 3: Passive attention-getting activities may also be either constructive or destructive.

There are two types of passive attention-getting mechanisms as well as two types of active attention-getting mechanisms. Some children find passive attention-getting mechanisms more successful. The *passive-constructive* attention-seeking child is the charmer. He doesn't necessarily act constructively; he just sits there being charming and cute.

On the other hand, the *passive-constructive* child gains attention through laziness. When he doesn't do what he is supposed to do, mother and father are constantly trying to notice and encourage him (or they criticize and/or punish him). Either way the child gets the desired attention. The passive-destructive behavior is illustrated in the following story:

Paul is 16 years old and he is so lazy. Every morning I have to call him ten times to get him out of bed, and then he is so rushed I have to wait on him hand and foot or he'll be late to school. And, he always procrastinates his homework, and I have to remind him over and over again. I spend more time on him than my younger children.

Idea No. 4: The second goal of misbehavior is to dominate.

The second goal of misbehavior is to dominate. The child looks at the mother and father and thinks, "What really makes Mom and Dad what they are is that they have power over me. Power is what I need to be accepted." The child then attempts to exert power over his parents, as when the parents say, "You will," and the child retorts, "I won't." Parents can usually recognize when they are engaged in a power struggle because they feel anger toward the child.

The narrative below illustrates the goal to dominate or obtain power.

Dad: Bob, you're home late again. Haven't I told you that if you stay out past 11 p.m., you will not be able to drive the car anymore?

Bob   If I can't use the car, then maybe I just won't come home at all.

Dad: You will come home, and you will get here on time!

Bob: I will not, and you can't make me!

Idea No. 5: The third goal of misbehavior is power.

The third goal of misbehavior is power which is associated with active- and passive-destruction methods. Although power and revenge are possible by constructive "deeds," this is rare in children. A child actively seeking power through destructive tactics is a rebel and does the opposite of what is expected. The passive-destructive power seeker is not the rebel type but rather shows his power by being stubborn and refusing to submit to the power of others.

Idea No. 6: The fourth goal of misbehavior is revenge.

A revengeful child is one who has lost in the power game and feels humiliated. He sees he is not strong enough to compete with his more powerful parents or teacher. To belong, he feels he must hurt the parents or teacher as much as they have hurt him; even an antagonist belongs. The revengeful child does not concern himself with the consequences of his actions—he is only interested in hurting.

Active-destructive children seeking revenge will usually retaliate physically. They break Mother's cherished music box, cut the curtains, or poke holes in the couch. These children are also oblivious to the possible consequences. The passive-destructive "revengers" employ less physical means. They no longer hope for attention or power but feel that finding their place in the family means making themselves hated. They know how to hurt and take advantage of others' vulnerabilities, embarrassment, or shame.

Idea No. 7: The fifth goal of misbehavior is helplessness.

The fifth goal of misbehavior is helplessness. The child may, when asked to do something, pretend illness or inability to accomplish the task. At this point the child becomes so discouraged that he feels it is probably better not to do anything than to face the possible consequences of failing or losing; anything he does will probably be met by criticism and ridicule. The following dialogue illustrates this idea:

Mother:	Ann, please put this coat away.
Ann:	I don't know where it goes.
Mother:	Put it in the hall closet.
Ann:	Which one?
Mother:	The one closest to the door.
Ann:	I can't, there's no hanger.
Mother:	Find one in the other closet.
Ann:	I can't find one.

This sequence of communications could go on indefinitely.

Hopefully, your child will never be in the next stage or goal of behavior which is helplessness. Here the child simply gives up. To avoid all these stages the use of *encouragement* is necessary.

In theory, not rewarding should be the most effective way of eliminating behavior, for no behavior continues unless it is reinforced. The key to using this intervention technique is in identifying when and where the reinforcement for undesirable behaviors occurs. Once these reinforcers have been identified, it is usually easy to eliminate them. Within a matter of days, behavior should weaken and then disappear.

Now you have an opportunity to use your creativity in completing Learning Experience 23.1.

LEARNING EXPERIENCE 23.1

Self-Test on Eliminating Undesirable Behavior

Circle "T" for True or "F" for False to each of the following statements about eliminating undesirable behavior.

1. T F The simplest way to eliminate negative behavior is to not reward it.

2. T F Children often misbehave because they want and get attention.

3. T F The attention-seeking child seems to assume he is important only when attended to.

4. T F The child who does destructive activities will persist if given the attention he seeks.

5. T F The charmer gets attention by being charming and cute.

6. T F The lazy child will start working if you criticize and punish enough.

7. T F Lazy children who don't get up in time for school and don't get their homework done in time should be reminded over and over and helped to get everything done so they will do well in school.

8. T F Parents who are engaged in a power struggle with their children are often angry with the child.

9. T F Power struggles between adults and children teach children that power is very important.

10. T F The passive-destructive power-seeker shows his power by being stubborn and refusing to submit to the power of others.

Principle 24

Encouraging the positive will teach new ways of doing things: substitute #1 for punishment.

Mother walked into young Mary's bedroom and the child announced that she has made her own bed this morning. However, Mother only sees a pile of sheets covered by a not so neatly placed bedspread. She says, "That bed isn't made. You've just piled everything up. You go on outside and play and I'll make this bed for you.

Idea No. 1: Provide encouragement by eliminating discouragement.

In this case the mother has discouraged her daughter and has neglected giving credit where credit was due. She subtly told her daughter that she couldn't perform the task she had proudly presented for approval. It is more important to praise the child for the good than to point out the negative in a discouraging manner. Through encouragement a child will practice and improve in the tasks performed. If criticized and discouraged, he will see no reason to attempt the task on subsequent occasions. Compare the previous mother's handling of the situation with the situation below:

Suzanne: Mommy, come upstairs. I've got a surprise for you!

Mom: What is it, Suzie?

Suzanne: I made my bed this morning. Come see! (Mom goes upstairs)

Mom: I see a pile of bedclothes on the bed but I think you're not finished yet. Come, let's finish this together.

(Mom and Suzanne work on the bed together)

Mom: There, it's finished now and you did such a good job of helping. Do you think you can do it alone tomorrow?

Suzanne: I don't know. It takes a long time.

Mom: I know you can do it. Just do it like we did it together today.

Idea No. 2: There are at least four rules to follow when giving encouragement to children.

Four general rules should be considered when giving encouragement to children.

1. Accentuate the positive and eliminate the negative. Instead of saying, "Don't get water on the porch," say "Keep the water on the grass." To a timid child say, "It is nice that you are going to visit Aunt Hilda. She likes to talk with you and wants to hear what you have to say," not "People won't like you unless you talk to them; don't be shy and whisper; speak out loud."

2. Try to get the child to express his feelings. Ask the child, "How does that make you feel?" or, "What do you think about that?" This encourages the child to evaluate his performance. Sometimes children will be able to realistically judge what they did wrong themselves. Children should also be allowed to express their feelings about corrections or criticisms they may have received. If parents listen to children's feelings, they easily discover how the children feel and when they may have been harsh or unfair.

3. Be sincere. Sometimes a quick "That's nice, dear" is more discouraging than no comment at all. Parents should try to make a positive attempt to find something real to compliment or be honest in their lack of praise. In almost all situations, however, there is something positive that can be said. The danger in giving insincere praise is that it invalidates honest compliments given at other times.

4. Join in and do things together. Be positive while helping. If you can't join in then give a sincere word of encouragement to partial and small behaviors when the other person is trying.

In summary, behavior is goal-directed; family atmosphere and family constellation are significant influences on a person's lifestyle; misbehavior has a goal; and children should be given encouragement to help prevent misbehavior.

Now continue to Learning Experience 24.1.

LEARNING EXPERIENCE 23.1

Self-Test on Principle 24

Mark the answer that expresses how you feel about each statement below. (ANSWER KEY: 1=Rarely Agree; 2=Sometimes Agree; 3=Often Agree; 4=Usually Agree)

1. 1 2 3 4   Pointing out the negative is as equally important an instructional tool as praising a child for positive actions.

2. 1 2 3 4   The parent who sees that a child has not accomplished a task properly should work with the child and compliment what was done.

3. 1 2 3 4   A good slogan for encouraging good behavior is "Accentuate the positive and eliminate the negative."

4. 1 2 3 4   It is a good idea to try to help the child express how he feels about how he did the task.

5. 1 2 3 4   Children are often realistic judges of their behavior if they are asked to evaluate it.

6. 1 2 3 4   Children should be encouraged to express how they feel about their work and their behavior.

7. 1 2 3 4   Parents should compliment their children even when they do not feel that the behavior is worthy of compliments.

8. 1 2 3 4   Usually parents can find something positive to say about their children's behavior if they try hard enough.

9. 1 2 3 4   Misbehavior usually has a goal, and the usual goal is attention.

10. 1 2 3 4   Instruction ahead of time helps the child achieve and makes giving encouragement afterwards more possible.

SUMMARY

Instructions: Mark *a* if the statement is true and *b* if it is false.

1. The most documented principle in psychology is "rewards work."

2. Fortunately rewards do not require long-term objectives and planning.

3. In a basic sense, rewards mean giving things to children when they do what is right.

4. Even though punishment does not have an immediate effect, most parents like to use it.

5. Punishment may actually make a child's behavior less predictable.

6. The first goal of misbehavior is revenge.

7. If one understands the goal of a child misbehavior then a parent can more intelligently react and find ways to eliminate or reduce the misbehavior.

8. The four general rules to encourage children are: 1) accentuate the positive and eliminate the negative, 2) try to get the child to express feelings, 3) be sincere, 4) do things together.

9. It is important to compliment children, and parents can usually find a way to compliment if they try hard enough.

10. Construction and planning ahead of time will enable the parent to provide encouragement in situations where discouragement and negative experiences frequently occur.

LESSON SIX

Substitutes for Punishment

After you have successfully completed this lesson, you should be able to do the following:

1. Describe effective substitutes for punishment.

2. Apply and use five substitutes for punishment to reduce or eliminate unwanted behavior.

3. Make and apply natural consequences in a family setting.

4. Apply logical consequences in a family setting.

Principle 25

You can't do good and bad at the same time.

During the summer, I worked at a summer camp for kids from low- income groups in the Los Angeles area. Many of the boys that came to camp were quite aggressive and often started fights with the other boys in the cabins. It was invariably very hot throughout the day, so a favorite activity was to go swimming in the pool. When a boy did something nice for one of the other boys, such as doing his clean-up duty, I gave him extra time in the pool while everyone else stood there in the heat watching him. Helping behaviors were positively reinforced, and it was amazing how fast the other kids caught on and stopped fighting.

Idea No. 1: The most effective way of eliminating bad behavior is to teach good behavior.

The summer camp counselor in the above example rewarded cooperative behavior rather than punishing aggressive behavior. The success of this method depends on increasing the occurrence of a desirable behavior through rewards making it impossible to perform the undesired behavior.

Idea No. 2: There are two questions to ask to determine a way to use the incompatible response principle.

The key to eliminating undesirable behavior is to reinforce desirable behaviors incompatible with the undesirable one. Smiling is incompatible with frowning. Laughing is incompatible with crying. Telling the truth is incompatible with lying; sharing is incompatible with selfishness; and courtesy is incompatible with rudeness. To select an incompatible desirable behavior, ask the following questions:

1. Is there a behavior that is the opposite of the undesired response?

2. When he/she performs this preferred behavior, will it be impossible for him/her to perform the undesired behavior?

In a preschool classroom a four-year old girl isolated herself from the other children and received adult attention for this behavior. The incompatible response in this case is obvious. Instead of trying to eliminate withdrawal, the teacher should attempt to increase the child's social interaction. In this case, the teacher ignored any isolated behavior and rewarded the girl when peer play was initiated. Since peer interactions did not occur frequently, anything close to a peer interaction had to be initially reinforced; even standing near or playing decide another child was reinforced. Gradually, social interaction began to occur. This child acquired an acceptable level of social interaction within one month.[61]

Complete Learning Experiences 26.1 and 26.2 to learn how to use this very powerful substitute for punishment.

LEARNING EXPERIENCE 25.1

Teaching Good Behavior to Eliminate Bad Behavior

A very positive method of reducing bad behavior is to teach children good behavior to replace the undesired behavior. How do you feel about each of the statements below? Discuss any of the items that you disagree or strongly disagree with. **(ANSWER KEY: SA=Strongly Agree; A=Agree; NS=Not Sure; D=Disagree; SD=Strongly Disagree)**

1. A good idea for eliminating fighting is to reward children for being cooperative.

    SA   A   NS   D   SD

2. When a child says something unkind, a parent should respond by smiling and saying something kind.

    SA   A   NS   D   SD

3. One mother tried to eliminate selfish behavior by rewarding those who voluntarily shared cookies and other treats with other children in the family.

    SA   A   NS   D   SD

4. When one girl in the family had a problem with not washing her hair, Mother taught all the girls how to cut and trim hair, and how to style it.

    SA   A   NS   D   SD

5. Bob had a problem with hitting and picking on his little brothers and sisters, so Mother got karate lessons for the younger children.

    SA   A   NS   D   SD

6. Philip cried easily, so whenever he cried Mother told him jokes and repeated them again and again until he laughed.

    SA   A   NS   D   SD

Principle 26

Time-outs from fun and frustration: substitute #2 for punishment

A frustrated father described a successful solution to a conflict with his son:

When I was watching a basketball game two Sundays ago my little boy was making a fuss about eating his dinner. He was arguing loudly with my wife so I asked him to be quiet and finish his dinner. He continued to howl so I quickly and unceremoniously took him to his time-out area (his room), and told him that when he could be quiet he could join us again. It worked.

Idea No. 1: Time-outs help children solve problems themselves.

When using a time-out procedure, the child is removed from the environment or activity in which the undesirable behavior is occurring. This procedure is not considered punishment in the sense that an aversive stimulus is not administered to stop the behavior. Rather, this procedure involves removing all positive reinforcers of the behavior, and placing the child in a "time-out" room or setting void of attention, toys, and other positive stimuli. Many instructional settings have rooms designated as "time-out rooms" where people are placed for specified periods of time until they can return and manage their behavior properly. The time-out room should not be so attractive that the child likes being sent to time-out.

Idea No. 2: Usually time-outs are arranged so that all positive elements are removed from the location.

There is another kind of time-out that is rarely used or noticed. It is positive and very surprising. One mother uses it all the time. Here is what she did yesterday:

Her young son was acting just terrible. He wanted his way and in her mind deserved to be punished. Just as she was going to take some privileges away, she had a change of heart. She knew her son hadn't gotten enough sleep the night before and she had been very busy with other things all morning. Suddenly, she said, "Come here" and held out her arms. The boy was a little befuddled and hesitated until she said, "I want to hold you." He came and for a few minutes she rocked him in the rocking chair. There were no more problems for the rest of the day.

Now, this is not the usual time-out, but it was a time-out from what was going on and it was a time-out that worked. Maybe children don't like a time-out from fun, but maybe they sometimes need, as do adults, a time-out from frustration and a time-out to catch up on some attention and affection.

Proceed now to Learning Experiences 26.1.

LEARNING EXPERIENCE 26.1

Using Time-Outs to Solve Problems

Circle the answer that most clearly defines your opinion/ understanding of the statement. (**ANSWER KEY: SA=Strongly Agree; A=Agree; NS=Not Sure; D=Disagree; SD=Strongly Disagree**)

1. A time-out room is an effective tool to motivate positive behavior.

    SA   A   NS   D   SD

2. A time-out room is most effective when it is void of attention, toys, and other positive stimuli.

    SA   A   NS   D   SD

3. A time-out room should not be so attractive that the child likes being sent to time-out.

    SA   A   NS   D   SD

4. Another time-out that is effective with a very young child is just holding and rocking the child.

    SA   A   NS   D   SD

5. I feel that using "time-out" is more effective than punishment.

    SA   A   NS   D   SD

Principle 27

Changing the environment changes behavior: substitute #3 for punishment.

My grandson was a lively little preschooler who seemed to be in perpetual motion. He dumped the contents of many kitchen and bathroom cabinets each day. Instead of screaming at him to stop, his mother put child-proof latches on all the cabinets and the behavior stopped.

Sometimes behavior is a result of or at least partly caused by the environment. Often the behavior does not change unless we change the environment. Most families do not have the luxury of moving to a new neighborhood as in the following story, but a change of friends is another way to change the environment.

Idea No. 1: An easy solution to undesirable behavior may be to change the stimulus.

Fortunately, many problems are less serious and can be solved by less drastic means. Some behaviors seem to be related to specific stimuli or conditions which are present when the responses occur. To change the response, it may simply be necessary to change the stimulus. For example, the child who is having nightmares may be reading violent comic books or watching scary television shows. The easiest solution may be to remove the comic books or television shows. Likewise, if your children always fight over a particular toy, it may work to simply remove that toy. It is discouraging to observe a mother continually scolding a child for getting into certain things, when it is easier and more effective to remove them from the child's reach.

The peer group has a strong impact on children, and too often undesirable behaviors are related to choices of friends. Parents may notice when, where, and with whom the child is playing when the undesirable behavior occurs, and restricting play with certain friends may eliminate the behavior.

Influencing a child's friends is quite difficult to do when they reach adolescence, but much can be done to directly and indirectly influence your child's choice of friends. Parents can select extra-curricular activities such as sports and music lessons which tend to attract like-minded parents and their children. Parents can strongly encourage academic pursuits since children who do well in school often have fewer behavior problems.

Parents can help children choose friends to take on special outings with the family. Parents can also talk to their children about the qualities they should look for in their friends. In more extreme cases parents have been known to send their children to summer camp or to visit grandparents as a means of removing them from an unhealthy environment which is eliciting undesirable behavior.

Idea No. 2: Parents can do many things to influence their children regarding choices of friends.

With older children parents have much less influence over choice of friends but they still need not support poor choices or supply the child with cars and money to run with a fast crowd or do things of which the parents do not approve. Undesirable friends often bring grief into our children's lives as well as into ours as shown by the stories below:

My son Brent lost interest in school and started hanging out with a rough crowd and began to get very poor grades. He did, however, have a good job and spent all of his money on an expensive stereo system which he bought piece by piece as he could afford them. When we went on vacation that summer our home was burglarized and my son's prized stereo system was stolen. The police investigated and said that the facts indicated that it was probably an inside job--done by one of my son's own friends who knew what he owned. We never did recover the stereo system, but my son did change friends.

Idea No. 3: Undesirable friends impact older teens negatively, but sometimes the child will change friends on his own to avoid future problems and to simplify his/her life.

Mark was always a good kid, but then he made friends with some new kids in our neighborhood. I didn't approve of their language, clothing, or behavior but nothing I said to Mark would dissuade him from his new friendships. One day my worst fears were realized--Mark was arrested for shoplifting. He claimed that he didn't really do it but that he just went along with his friends who did all the stealing.

Unfortunately for Mark, he had just had his eighteenth birthday while his friends were still only 17 years old. Therefore, Mark was tried as an adult, received a substantial fine, and even spent some time in jail. He was really upset by the whole experience and soon found some new friends who were more law-abiding and were interested in scholarship and school activities.

When trying to change the environment, the parent may want to consider one or more of the following:

1. Friends

2. Crowded rooms

3. Amount of time in contact with a sibling

4. Sending the child to live with someone else

5. Changing the music in the home or the child's room

6. Regulating the television programs the child watches

7. Eating meals together and spending more time together

8. Visiting new places

9. Enrolling child in new sports or activities or camps

10. Taking the child to church

11. Changing, redecorating rooms

The list is almost endless. Continue now with Learning Experiences 27.1.

LEARNING EXPERIENCE 27.1

Changing Behavior by Changing the Environment

Circle the answer you choose to respond to the statement. **(ANSWER KEY: SA=Strongly Agree; A=Agree; NS=Not Sure; D=Disagree; SD=Strongly Disagree)**

1. Putting safety latches on doors, cupboards, etc. is a cop-out for people who want to avoid disciplining their children.

    SA   A   NS   D   SD

2. Changing friends often helps change behavior.

    SA   A   NS   D   SD

3. Scolding children for getting into things is recommended.

    SA   A   NS   D   SD

4. Changing stimuli or conditions which are present when the responses occur is often effective.

    SA   A   NS   D   SD

5. Parents have no influence over a child's choice of friends.

    SA   A   NS   D   SD

6. Parents can help children pick extra-curricular activities in which they will choose good friends.

    SA   A   NS   D   SD

7. Even when children make poor choices of friends, parents should support these poor choices with the money necessary to continue their child's involvement with the peer group.

    SA   A   NS   D   SD

8. Sometimes adversity (such as stealing of personal items) is needed for some youth to quit hanging-out with undesirable friends.

    SA   A   NS   D   SD

HOW TO SCORE THIS LEARNING EXPERIENCE: Give yourself 2 points for every "strongly disagree" and 1 point for every "disagree" for ODD numbered questions. Give yourself 2 points for every "strongly agree" and 1 point for every "agree" for EVEN numbered questions.

TOTAL FOR ODD NUMBERED QUESTIONS: _____

TOTAL FOR EVEN NUMBERED QUESTIONS: _____

Principle 28

Rewarding for not acting bad: substitute #4 for punishment

I was a mother's helper for six months last year for a newborn baby and a four-and-a-half-year old. The four-and-a-half-year old would mess in his pants on purpose. We had the doctor check him out, but there was nothing physiologically wrong with him. He would do it for attention, so his mother and I promised him if he went for a week without messing in his pants, we could go to the zoo. Using this procedure, he immediately learned to handle the problem.

The technical name for this procedure is "Omission Training." You inform the child that if he refrains from an undesirable behavior he will be rewarded. Usually, this expectation must be specified in terms of time. Thus, a child can be told: "If I don't hear any arguing for the next half hour, then we will all go to town and have a treat." In omission training, the child is expected to discontinue a response for a period of time. As an example, consider the disruptive behavior of an elementary school child. The teacher reinforced non-disruptive behavior by delaying recess until no disruption occurred for ten minutes. If disruptive behavior occurred during the ten minutes, then the children would have to wait another ten minutes.

Idea No. 1: Use omission training by rewarding a child for not acting bad (a specific act) for a certain period of time.

An extreme example of omission training was used to eliminate self- injurious behavior of institutionalized retarded children. Behaviors included face-scratching, eye-poking, and head-banging. Although several procedures were tried, omission training was effective in eliminating these injurious behaviors by withholding food and then reinforcing with food when the behavior did not take place.

Sometimes omission training attempts can even be humorous as in the case cited below of a frustrated single parent:

My 16-year-old daughter is very conscious of her surroundings especially where we live. She believes that if I were to get married, we would move from this apartment which she calls a "pit" and live like so- called "normal people." However, due to her being an only child, she is jealous of anyone who may direct my attention away from her, especially when it comes to men. Whenever I am with a male companion she is obnoxious. She screams and hangs out the window and says things like, "What are you doing out there?" or "When are you coming in?" So, one evening I told her that if she wouldn't behave that way I would date. Her hope is that if I date enough, I'll eventually get married; therefore, she stopped her childish behavior because she knew only through my dating were we ever going to live like "normal people."

In natural, more common situations, this omission procedure is frequently used. Mother may say that if there is no loud talk or disruptive noise at the dinner table, she will serve a special dessert. A father may say, "If you children can be quiet and not fight with each other so I can get my work done this morning, then we'll go to the park this afternoon."

Idea No. 2: Rewards for not acting badly are commonly offered by parents in natural situations.

Proceed with Learning Experiences 28.1

LEARNING EXPERIENCE 28.1

Rewarding Children for Not Acting Badly

Fill in the blanks:

1. Omission training involves rewarding a child for not acting_____.

2. In omission training the child is expected to_____ (continue or discontinue) a response for a period of time.

3. Non-disruptive behavior can be reduced by delaying a reward until no disruptions occur for a specific period of_____.

4. In severe cases, omission training may be done by using_____ to deprive and reward the targeted behavior.

5. Parents may reward non-disruptive behavior with special _____to eat or special activities such as.

6. I can think of other incentives to use in encouraging children to avoid bad behaviors including_____.

7. My opinion about using omission training (or incentives to not act badly) is_____.

Principle 29

Nobody likes too much of one thing: substitute #5 for punishment.

Sometimes we hear the expression, "Too much of a good thing." A child may say: "I'm tired of it;" "We do that all the time;" "Not that again;" or "Let's do something else" Even if a child really likes something, if he gets too much he usually doesn't like it anymore. This concept is called "satiation." Reinforcing properties of rewards are lost with excessive quantity.

Idea No. 1: When children get too much of something they usually like it less.

Closely related to satiation is negative practice. When this method is used, a person is asked to practice or perform the unwanted behavior again and again. This could apply to nail-biting, stammering, thumb-sucking, swearing, and other types of annoying behaviors. So, you can either present the *stimulus* over and over as in satiation or require the *response* over and over as in negative practice.

An example involved a young lady who reported how she came to dislike an activity as a result of satiation.

I was a tomboy while in grade school. I wanted a Johnny Bench Pitchback for elementary school graduation. My parents didn't want to get it for me because they thought it would foster my boyish characteristics, but they got it for me nevertheless. I soon stopped using it as much but my mother would always say, "You complained to get it, now use it." After being forced to play with it day after day, I had only one solution—I broke it.

Idea No. 2: Too much of an activity or negative practice also makes it less attractive to the child or adolescent.

A word of caution should be given at this point.. Obviously, common sense would require that for some things such as drugs or sex, negative practice or satiation would not be appropriate. As in all things, and for all these principles, there is a "time and place to *DO* things" and a "time and place *NOT TO DO* things." There is no substitute for good judgment and trusting your positive instincts.

Now, continue with Learning Experiences 29.1

LEARNING EXPERIENCE 29.1

Self-Evaluation on Satiation and Negative Practice Concepts

Answer each of the following questions. For questions 1, 2, and 5 write in the appropriate responses. For questions 3 and 4 circle the appropriate letter for your answer.

1. The two main ideas or methods associated with this principle are:

   a.

   b.

2. I regard this principle as:

   a. Exceptionally valuable

   b. Very valuable

   c. Valuable

   d. Somewhat valuable

   e. Not valuable

3. When it comes to putting this principle into action in my family, I feel:

   a. Exceptionally confident

   b. Very confident

   c. Confident

   d. Somewhat confident

   e. Not confident

List below any actions you can take to gain confidence and put this principle into practice in your family life.

Principle 30

Using natural consequences

My little brother was destructive when he was small. He would take expensive toys and roll them down the big avenue gutters soon to be lost forever. He would find ways to tear apart stuffed dolls and animals, or throw balls and other objects on buildings. One day he demolished his tricycle with a hammer. After much money was spent on toys, my parents decided not to replace them. My brother became somewhat distressed because his toys were slowly declining in number. He finally ended up not having any playthings. My parents didn't buy him toys until six months later when they bought him a brand new bike with training wheels. To this day (15 years later) that bike is still in the family. family.

Parents who rush out and replace the lost or ruined toys miss a great teaching opportunity.

Idea No. 1: Use natural consequences whenever possible.

When I was five years old I received a $5.00 bill for Christmas. I was so happy when I thought about all the things I would buy with that money. I played and played with my money. When we went to the store, my Mother asked to hold it for me so I would not lose it, but I wanted to play with it some more. She talked to me about not being careless with money, but I did not listen. So, I lost the money and someone took that money. In later years I thought of how sad it was to lose my money and I have tried to be very careful with my money.

It is often not necessary to physically or verbally punish a child in order for him or her to learn a very effective lesson. Just allow the child to bear the consequences of his undesirable behavior, and that will be an effective lesson. This concept of natural and logical consequences is here credited to the famous psychiatrist R. Dreikurs as referenced 62,63,64,65.

Idea No. 2: Usually parents should not protect their children from negative outcomes of the child's own mistakes.

It is often very difficult for parents to let children discover things for themselves, but sometimes a child has to learn a lesson involving an unwanted risk. The parents of the following child allowed him to learn for himself the consequences of his actions:

When I was in high school my parents were quite protective of my inappropriate behavior, i.e., bailing me out of jail when I was in trouble, seeing that I was cared for when I was drunk, or making sure I was okay when I arrived home late. They had come to the detention home several times to rescue me from the law. One day, without warning, my parents didn't come to my rescue when I got into trouble. I spent several nights in detention. I suffered and felt somewhat rejected. I decided the so-called "good times" I was having weren't worth the consequences.

Idea No. 3: If the child has done something that is breaking the law. It is usually not wise to interfere with the punishment already set up by the legal system for such behavior.

One Christmas when I was eleven years old and we didn't have much money, I shoplifted about $25 worth of scarves and jewelry. The police asked my Mom how she would like to handle this and I found myself hand-cuffed and riding in the squad car to the police station. Then my mom was also given the choice of whether I would have to report regularly to a probation officer. I never did any more shoplifting. Some older girls in my neighborhood never had to wear handcuffs, go to the police station to see the juvenile officer because their parents took care of everything. And, they did lots of shoplifting because nothing ever happened to them.

In this case, the parent had the choice of having nothing happen to the child, but she chose to have the child face the consequences of the act.

Idea No. 4: Parents who make excuses for their children and do not allow their children to suffer natural consequences at school limit the ability of schools to maintain order.

In the school setting, punishment is often avoided by children whose parents actually do the homework or write excuses that are not truthful or object to the punishment.

A school teacher writes the following:

It is really difficult to have any discipline in the schools today. If a child misbehaves I often cannot keep him in from recess because a parent will object to his lack of fresh air or keep him after school because it will inconvenience the parent or interfere with some recreational activity the parent has planned for the child. Also, when there are special treats brought in by parents, I must be sure that I do not deprive the child whose parents brought the treat no matter how inappropriate his or her behavior.

Also, I know that some of my students do not do their homework and their parents do it for them so their children will not get bad grades. This misses the whole purpose of homework.

A school principal describes his dilemma below:

Our high school has a very difficult problem with truancy and tardiness. We have tried everything, but an excessive number of students are always out in the halls and in the commons when they should be in class. The teachers mark them tardy and absent, and these lower their grades after three tardies or absences, but the parents write notes saying they were sick or at a doctor's office in order get them out of the absence or tardy. We know the parents are lying to protect their children, but there is nothing we can do. So, we live with our halls and commons full of students.

Idea No. 5: Wise parents carefully consider which consequences they should step in to save their children from natural consequences.

Trying to find a balance between expecting too much and expecting too little requires a great amount of sensitivity on a parent's part, but children should be allowed the privilege of failure. If a child is trying to climb up on to a chair and it doesn't look like he's going to make it, parents shouldn't run over and help him up. He should be allowed the experience of a failure, though being encouraged at the same time: "You almost made it that time, maybe you can do it next time." With that kind of approach a child is going to go back and try again by himself because he has been told he might be able to accomplish the task.

On the other hand, if the child is trying to do something that is dangerous such as jumping off stairs or a balcony, the parent should protect the child. Of course, if the child is trying to drive an automobile under age, the parent should protect both the child and other people that he/she might endanger by such actions.

Wise parents are sensible in loving their children enough to let them learn from their own mistakes when it is prudent to do so.

Go now to Learning Experiences 30.1.

LEARNING EXPERIENCE 30.1

Teaching with Natural Consequences

Circle the answer that describes most accurately your feelings about each statement. (**ANSWER KEY: SA=Strongly Agree; A=Agree; NS=Not Sure; D=Disagree; SD=Strongly Disagree**)

1. A child who destroys or loses his toys learns best if they are not replaced.

     SA   A   NS   D   SD

2. A child who is careless with money learns best to be careful with money when he loses it.

     SA   A   NS   D   SD

3. Teenagers who do things that are against the law learn quicker if their parents do not rescue them from punishment by the legal system.

     SA   A   NS   D   SD

4. Parents sometimes prevent their children from learning by cushioning the blow or removing the consequences entirely.

     SA   A   NS   D   SD

5. Criminal misdeeds by young children are less likely to continue if the children are allowed to suffer the consequences.

     SA   A   NS   D   SD

6. Parents should support the schools in disciplining their children.

     SA   A   NS   D   SD

7. Even if it results in lower grades, parents should not write notes to cover for children who skip classes.

     SA   A   NS   D   SD

8. Finding a balance between helping a child too much or too little is difficult.

     SA   A   NS   D   SD

9. A child should be allowed the privilege of failure at times instead of always being saved from his mistakes.

    SA   A   NS   D   SD

10. If a child is trying to do something dangerous, the parent should try to protect the child.

    SA   A   NS   D   SD

11. A child who is trying to drive a car when he is under age should be stopped not only for his own protection but for the protection of others.

    SA   A   NS   D   SD

Principle 31

Logical consequences

Idea No. 1: Logical consequences are useful when natural consequences are too dangerous.

Sometimes natural consequences are too dangerous, so logical consequences may be devised (e.g., a consequence that relates to the act but is not dangerous). Natural consequences usually occur without any intrusion by parents or care givers, whereas logical consequences are calculated beforehand. For example, if a child is continually running out into the street, a parent could not risk letting the natural consequences occur. A parent cannot let him run into the street, get hit by a car, and then say, "Now let that be a lesson to you!" Logical consequences are necessary in this case. "You may either play in the backyard or come in the house." A three-year-old child, for example, is not mature enough to assume responsibility for playing in the front yard unsupervised, so you let him choose the backyard or the house.

Idea No. 2: If children understand the logical consequences of their actions they are more likely to willingly accept the consequences.

A parent must help the child realize that consequences are the result of the child's misbehavior, not the parent's wishes. During this time, a parent can remain friendly and undisturbed. For example, one child was given the assignment of cleaning the kitchen before going to the beach. The child wandered off and did not attend to his chores. As the child repeatedly came back and asked when they were going to leave for the beach, the father calmly replied, "As soon as we get the work done, we can go." This child never completed the work, and as a result the trip was canceled without protest from the child.

To work best, logical consequences must be related to what the child has done. Punishment, on the other hand, may have no relationship to anything the child has done. A child does not do his chores and he gets spanked—the relationship between neglect of duties and spanking is not natural, but contrived, and the child fails to learn natural and logical connections between events. If, however, chores must be done before fun and games, the connection between failure to do work and deprivation of privileges fits together more logically.

Natural and logical consequences do not humiliate or pass moral judgments on the child. The child pays a price, but the parent is not the judge meting out the sentence. The word "wrong" need not be used. It is better if parents do not even emphasize the consequences but let them take place with as little involvement on their part as possible

Idea No. 3: Logical consequences do not flow naturally from the misbehavior but are logically connected to it unlike punishment which may be unrelated to the misbehavior.

It may appear that using natural and logical consequences is simply a form of punishment, but this is not the case. The difference between using natural and logical consequences and using punishment is not so much in terms of the actual impact on the child but in the way it is interpreted. Natural and logical consequences are not arbitrarily imposed by parents for the purpose of inflicting pain to reduce misbehavior. Instead, they are natural and logical consequences that apply to everyone living in the same environment. Instead of being vindictive, the parent can be compassionate, kind, and supportive in helping the child face consequences of his or her behavior.

Turn now to Learning Experiences 31.1.

LEARNING EXPERIENCE 31.1

For each of the statements below indicate your level of agreement by writing in the blank space one of the following numbers: **1=Strongly Agree; 2=Agree; 3=Undecided; 4=Disagree; 5=Strongly Disagree**

1. _____ Rewards work.

2. _____ Talking with children about problem behavior is usually a waste of time.

3. _____ Verbal praising of desired behavior should be used after the inappropriate behavior disappears.

4. _____ Punishment should match the misbehavior and be understood by the child.

5. _____ Too much punishment may interrupt the parent-child relationship.

6. _____ Physical punishment should almost never be used.

7. _____ Punishment may have unintended negative consequences.

8. _____ Physical punishment has an immediate effect.

9. _____ The first goal of misbehavior is attention-getting.

10. _____ An example of passive-destructive attention- getting is laziness or not getting work done.

11. _____ An example of active-destructive attention- getting is the charmer.

12. _____ Encouragement should emphasize the positive and eliminate the negative.

13. _____ Praise that is insincere is still better than no praise.

14. _____ Parents should teach good behavior that can crowd out bad behavior.

15. _____ Eliminating undesirable behaviors is best done by replacing them with incompatible good behaviors.

16. _____ Time-out involves placing a child in a new setting void of attention, toys, and other positive stimuli.

17. _____ Parents should leave choice of friends up to their children.

18. _____ The easiest solution to undesirable behavior may be to remove the stimulus.

19. _____ Omission training involves rewarding cessation of bad behaviors.

20. _____ Satiation or too much of something often eliminates the bad behavior.

21. _____ Letting children suffer natural consequences often eliminates undesirable behavior.

22. _____ Children need supportive parents who will do their homework for them and write excuses when they are truant.

23. _____ Logical consequences is another name for punishment.

24. _____ Parents can be compassionate and supportive in helping children face consequences.

25. _____ Natural consequences flow naturally from behavior, but logical consequences are connected to the behavior in a logical way.

SUMMARY

Instructions: Mark *a* if the statement is true and *b* if it is false

1. The most effective way of eliminating bad behavior is to teach good behavior.

2. Typically using time out to remove the child from where the unwanted behavior occurred and also removing positive elements is an effective way to remove unwanted behavior.

3. When changing the environment to change behavior, there is usually a very limited number of things that can be changed.

4. Omission training is a method of punishment where there is no reward.

5. Omission training should be used rarely and only when nothing else works.

6. When children get too much of something they usually like it less.

7. There is no downside or danger in using satiation or too much of one thing.

8. There are many substitutes to use when one does not want to punish.

9. It is possible to use more than one substitute or punishment at one time.

10. Of all of the substitutes for punishment, the incompatible response, or rewarding a child for doing the opposite of an unwanted response, is best.

11. Logical consequences means letting mother nature do the rewarding and punishment.

12. Parents should not protect their children from the negative outcomes of children's mistakes.

13. When a child breaks a law and is in trouble with the law or makes mistakes at school, the parent should not try to excuse them and protect them from the consequences.

14. Letting children experience natural consequences depends on the age of the child.

15. Finding a balance between helping a child too much or too little is difficult.

16. Logical consequences are especially helpful when natural consequences are too dangerous.

17. Logical consequences should be a retaliation or punishment.

18. Providing the child choices is important when using logical consequences.

19. When using logical consequences it is good to empathize with the child.

20. Logical consequences and punishment often are the same event, but the critical difference is how they are interpreted and used.

LESSON SEVEN

The Advantages of Using Low Power Techniques

After you have successfully completed this lesson, you should be able to do the following:

1. Appreciate and realize the advantages of using low power discipline techniques with young and older children.

2. Discuss how to influence behavior in a positive way with "I" messages.

3. Teach children to use both self- and other-oriented induction as a basis for moral action.

Principle 32

Use as low power as possible

I taught a brother and sister who were very disruptive— laughing and whispering, and tickling each other. They were not paying attention to the lesson, and I repeatedly requested them to behave and listen. This was totally ineffective. If I separated them, it seemed only to increase the disturbance by spreading it out. The situation turned into a battle to see who was stronger—me or the two children.

As a teacher, I was becoming very discouraged. My dealing with the situation was ineffective and problems seemed to be getting worse. Finally, one week I stopped right in the middle of the lesson, and closed my book, and began putting my pictures away. They noticed and asked me what I was doing. I explained to them that since they didn't seem to listen, they must not want to hear the lesson. I told them that it was discouraging to me to take the time to prepare the lesson, and then to come and have nobody listen. I wasn't going to do it anymore. This really got their attention, and they said they wanted to hear. After this meaningful and serious discussion, they seemed to understand my point of view, and while they are not perfect children, the class is now manageable.

Idea No. 1: Use the least amount of power necessary to accomplish the task.

We want to emphasize the advantages of using as little power as possible. Don't give all your power away and have no influence. Certainly, it is understandable that you should use whatever power and influence you have to maintain your standards. But, if you can do this with less power and force, why not try the low power methods. For our purposes, we will find that using a more powerful incentive to deter or stop an action actually increases the desire.

Idea No. : 2 Use as little power as possible.

The question of using power is probably the primary and the most enduring question facing parents. Yet, parents often underestimate how much power they possess when dealing with young children. The following is a list of some elements that give power to parents.

1. food and water

2. activities and opportunities

3. money and other socially attractive incentives

4. possession of information and knowledge

5. affection

6. love

7. pain

Idea No. :3 Parents control many elements which may be used to control or influence children.

When parents use one or more of these elements to control or influence their children, they are using power. Generally, the power can be classified into the following two divisions: reward power and punishment power. Research exists to show that both reward power and punishment power work. While reward and punishment power can be effective, there are disadvantages. Reliance on reward power also includes some of the same disadvantages and is also classified as a high-power technique.

Idea No: 4 There are some disadvantages to controlling children through high-power rewards.

There are some, not too serious, disadvantages in controlling children through high-power rewards. They are the following:

1. Children come to expect a payoff for their behavior.

2. Children stop behaving when rewards stop—sometimes with a strong negative reaction.

3. Parents lose ability to compete with other sources of reward, e.g., clubs, peers, etc.

4. Children develop the feeling that external causes (the rewards) rather than internal elements control their actions.

However, the above listings of disadvantages of high-reward power child-rearing techniques does not contain any especially negative elements, and each listing requires some qualification. All in all, using high-reward power is not too bad an approach.

Idea No. 5: Using reward power works but has some disadvantages.

Research indicates that if a parent wants to produce obedient children, the high power approach can be used. If you want children who are compliant, obedient, submissive, courteous, and proper with the least effort in the shortest time, then judiciously control and administer these reward powers. Give rewards only when the child acts in a way you desire. In fact, it is almost impossible to avoid using high reward power during the first two years when the children's communication skills are less developed and their comprehension limited.

One might ask, "If using high reward power is so effective, why not use it?" You might be saying, "I'll settle for a child like that!" However, upon further reflection, you will likely conclude that you want more than just obedience from your children--a higher goal is sought. You want them to be obedient for the right reasons not just to avoid your punishment or get your rewards. You want them to be obedient because they love you and they want to do what is right.

Idea No. 6: Many parents want more than obedience.

A higher goal is to facilitate a child's growth toward maturity. It is largely upon this change in goals that low-power techniques excel. Low-power techniques better facilitate the development of personal growth. While obedience during childhood may be compatible with personal growth towards maturity, there are reasons to believe that in many cases quickly-obtained obedience works against long-term growth.

When using low-power techniques, the child will not experience a powerful parent controlling rewards and punishments. Instead, he will perceive expectations from a responsible, warm, affectionate adult who not only trusts him, but also is ready to help. The parent becomes a helper, a growth facilitator, and a partner in growing rather than a domineering authority who assumes total responsibility for the child's growth.

As you might expect, children raised in such conditions are different. Findings from investigations of parent-child interactions and from descriptions of children from homes where parents use low-power techniques are now presented below. The findings describe basically children from homes using low power.

1. Positive

2. Independent

3. Self-sufficient

4. Assertive

5. Creative and able to solve novel problems

6. Self-motivated

It is often asserted that the primary advantages of low-power discipline is that it better prepares the child for the independence that comes with maturity. Upon comparison, 21-year-old children from homes using low power will be more independent and more mature than those from high-power homes. It is probably true that when using low power, children will not always come as promptly when called; they will not persist as long on a tiring, boring task; and they will make more mistakes in carrying out assignments. Also, the parent may feel more frustration and may not have as much control nor receive as much respect. However, what the parent does receive when using low-power techniques is likely more genuine, and enduring. Ways to do this will be discussed next but first complete Learning Experience 33.1.

LEARNING EXPERIENCE 32.1

Choosing the Best Reasons for Good Behavior

In this activity, you will choose the reasons for good behavior which appeal to you the most. "Why are you going home at midnight when you could just sneak in through the open window?" one adolescent asked another. Choose the answers which you would like your child to express. You may choose more than one.

1. Because I will get a licking if I don't.

2. Because I will get grounded if I don't.

3. Because if I do I get $50 at the end of the month.

4. Because I don't want my mother to worry.

5. Because I feel guilty when I sneak.

6. Because I promised my dad and I always keep my promises.

7. Because I had a big discussion with my parents about it and they moved my curfew   from 11:00 to 12:00 and I think that's fair.

8. Oh, I just like to get along with my parents.

Principle 33

Sharing feelings with "I" messages

In this example, Mr. H. simply shared his feelings and as a result, the children settled down. This is an example of a low power approach. They had not realized how their behavior and noise were affecting their father. When the impact of their behavior was pointed out to them, they were willing to act so that their father would not experience additional distress. In life, we all alter behavior because of its potential impact on others; this is also true of children. If used properly, sending "I" messages, or sharing feelings, will teach children how their behaviors affect other people. [66]

Idea No. 1: Sharing feelings helps children understand how their behaviors affect others.

Unfortunately, parents often underestimate children's willingness and ability to change behavior that is annoying to others. Instead, these parents tend to send solution messages to their children as mentioned before, such as: 1) ordering and directing; 2) warning and admonishing; and 3) preaching and moralizing. Three things are wrong with these messages. First, children don't like being told what to do. Second, they communicate that the child is incapable or you don't trust him. Third, it conveys to a child that you think your needs are more important than his.

Another ineffective method commonly used is a "put-down" message or "You" message. "Put-down" messages are statements such as "You're really a loser," or "You're no help," or "You better change; you're always messing things up."   They differ from "I" messages such as "I'm distressed when that happens," or "I'm worried about you at night," or "I'm afraid you're going to fall." Mr. H. shared his feelings about the children's noise in the back of the car by sending a series of "I" messages. An "I" message simply states how you feel or think about something. It presents the facts and the problem, and it is up to the other person to respond constructively. The parent does not tell the child exactly what to do. The child resolves the problem and then responds.

Idea No. 2: Sharing feelings through "I" messages have advantages over commands.

"I" messages are more effective for the following reasons:

They are less apt to provoke resistance and rebellion in the child. When a child hears a parent say, "I'm worried," resistance and rebellion are not usually engendered.

They are more effective because they place responsibility with the child. The parent identifies how the child's behavior is making the parent feel.

They help the child assume responsibility for his own behavior. When a "You" message is sent, the parent is assuming responsibility for the child's behavior through ordering, lecturing, judging, etc.

Because they are honest, they tend to encourage the child to send honest messages in return. [67]

Idea No. 3: "I" messages must be skillfully used.

When a parent sends "I" messages some traps need to be avoided. First, don't always send negative "I" messages. For example, when a child is out late at night, the parent can use positive statements, or at least include some positive elements such as "I'm so glad to see you return." "I" messages are often insufficiently stated. For example, if a child is playing in a dangerous area, the parent wouldn't say, "I'm worried." An "I" message should convey the true feeling: "I was so worried that I just couldn't..." or "I am extremely scared...." Emphasize the true strength of feelings, rather than sending weak messages.

Also, too many "I" messages may overwhelm the child. If the child continually hears, "I was worried, I was unhappy, I was afraid, I'm concerned, I'm questioning," day after day, he will become emotionally exhausted. Parents must learn to use this technique appropriately—in the right circumstances, and in the right "dosage."

The child may at first ignore "I" messages. In this case, the parent should send a second and perhaps much stronger message to be certain the child hears the source of concern.

Idea No. 4: "I" messages are effective, but they must be strong enough, used judiciously, and sometimes repeated.

The essential element which makes the sharing of feelings effective is trust--belief that children, when they are aware that they are disturbing, irritating, or annoying to other people, will self-correct the behavior. If they are never given the opportunity to self-correct, children will not learn consideration and responsibility. Sharing feelings provides the opportunity for a child to act responsibly for the welfare of others.

Idea No. 5: There are three parts to the "I" message.

The "I" contains three parts: a clear statement of how the parent feels; the child's behavior and why the behavior is upsetting to the parent

Idea No. 6: Feelings may be shared non-verbally.

Young children are sensitive to other people's feelings, Parenting so that parents can use nonverbal signals to share

Idea No. 7: Sharing feelings through "I" messages helps young children to learn to care about the feelings of others.

"I" messages do require some skill on the parent's part. When first used, they will sometimes fail to produce results because children have been so accustomed to other methods and have not learned to be sensitive and considerate of their parents. However, with continued use, this technique of sharing feelings will begin to yield success. To be effective, a parent must learn to avoid destructive communications and "phoniness" when communicating feelings.

Idea No. 8: Share positive feelings about good things that happen in family life.

It is important to remember that "I" messages should also be used when sharing positive feelings, not just when portraying a problem. Parents must express positive feelings to the child, explaining what the child did to make him that way. For example, "It feels so good to come home after each day, because the house always looks so good and you children are always so thoughtful and kind to me." Without question, it is better to have an abundance of positive feelings rather than negative, even though "I" messages may be used effectively in negative instances.

Please complete Learning Experiences 33.1, 33.2.

LEARNING EXPERIENCE 33.1

Self-Test on Sharing Feelings

Circle the answer that describes most nearly your response to the following statements. (**ANSWER KEY: SA=Strongly Agree; A=Agree; NS=Not Sure; D=Disagree; SD=Strongly Disagree**)

1. Children can and will alter their behavior because of its potential impact on others.

    SA   A   NS   D   SD

2. Sending "I" messages or sharing feelings will teach children how their behaviors affect other people.

    SA   A   NS   D   SD

3. Parents often underestimate children's willingness and ability to change behavior that is annoying to others.

    SA   A   NS   D   SD

4. Solving children's problems for them is not the best way to help children.

    SA   A   NS   D   SD

5. "I" messages are more effective for improving children's behavior because they are less apt to provoke resistance and rebellion in the child.

    SA   A   NS   D   SD

6. Placing responsibility on the child is more effective in changing children's behavior.

    SA   A   NS   D   SD

7. Parents who honestly express their feelings encourage children to send honest messages in return.

    SA   A   NS   D   SD

8. "I" messages are more effective if some are positive messages rather than all negative messages.

SA   A   NS   D   SD

9. Too many "I" messages may overwhelm the child, so parents need to use the technique appropriately.

SA   A   NS   D   SD

10. The essential element which makes sharing of feelings effective is trust.

SA   A   NS   D   SD

11. When parents use "I" messages to share feelings, they have the opportunity to engage in problem-solving.

SA   A   NS   D   SD

12. Sharing feelings through "I" messages helps young children to learn to care about the feelings of others.

SA   A   NS   D   SD

13. Sharing feelings may also be done effectively in nonverbal ways, especially with young children.

SA   A   NS   D   SD

LEARNING EXPERIENCE 33.3

Sharing Feelings to Change Children's Behavior

Fill in the blanks in the following sentences:

1. Sharing feelings helps children _____ how their behaviors affect others.

2. The essential element that makes sharing of feelings effective is _____ .

3. A major benefit of sharing feelings with children is that it encourages the child to assume _____ for his own behavior.

4. It is important that not all "I" messages be negative; some messages should be _____.

5. Sharing feelings through "I" messages helps children change _____ better than solution messages such as ordering, directing, warning, and admonishing.

6. A "put-down" message is another _____ method of trying to change behavior.

Principle 34

Help children have feelings for self and others.

My mom consistently used feelings to communicate herself to me when I was an adolescent. On one particular occasion I had teased my youngest sister until she began to cry.

My mom took me aside and gently told me that my teasing bothered her as well, and that she thought my teasing might cause contention in the home because I wasn't showing respect to my sister as I should. What touched me the most about my mom's messages was the feeling she conveyed to me. I had no desire to see her feelings hurt from my misbehavior, so I improved my actions considerably. Though the temptation to tease still exists, I would rather maintain peace and harmony in the home.

Idea No. 2: Feeling techniques can be used for both negative and positive acts.

Consider some additional examples of inductive statements:

"When you forget to feed the dog, he will be hungry during the night."

If you wear your sister's clothes, she won't have anything clean to wear when she comes home from school."

"I have been waiting here for one hour and am very bored. You said you would meet me at two o'clock and it's already three."

These statements are intended to produce either an understanding or an emotional response for the act being discussed. However, they need not always focus on the negative. For example, a parent might say:

"Look at your brother. Now that you let him ride your bicycle, see how happy he is."

"Don't you feel better now that you have completed your assignment."

Idea No. 3: Feelings are often very powerful and can change behavior.

Explaining feelings is often powerful enough to change behavior, as was emphasized in the previous section on sharing feelings. One student recounted the following incident:

When I was in high school I started dating a pretty rowdy guy whom my parents disapproved of very much. However, my dad could not convince me to quit dating him.

One night I came home very late after a date and my mom was still up. I asked her what she was doing up so late and she said she was worried about me. She then started crying.

She shared with me her feelings, expressing them in such a way that I later quit dating the guy. Mom's feelings changed my behavior.

Idea No. 4: Induction is not withdrawing love or using guilt.

Many similar statements used in induction might elicit guilt or self- condemnation, and are, therefore, not clearly differentiated from some other techniques discussed. For example, it is difficult to clearly separate the effects of withdrawing love, and rejecting or ignoring your child, from indicating your disappointment, or implying to the child that he ought to feel bad. All of these procedures have an element of both love withdrawal and induction. Many parents, when reasoning with their children, make it very clear that Mom and Dad were hurt or disappointed.

However, a discrimination can be made. Induction is a parental behavior indicating that others are hurt or disappointed, without suggesting that love and respect are being withdrawn. Induction involves drawing generalizations from actions or behavior rather than blaming the child. In addition, induction need not occur after a behavior but may occur in advance through discussion or vicarious experience.

Idea No. 5: Induction is effective for many reasons and helps the child develop empathy.

Why is induction effective? First, this technique explains the consequences of the child's behavior. Attention is directed away from a personal evaluation and is concerned with action rather than judgment of the child. In addition, induction teaches how to produce positive reactions or acts such as reparations or apologies. Induction helps motivate children to become more mature in the use of reasoning and discussion. It also communicates to the child that he is an individual capable of understanding more mature concepts, having the ability to give up personal satisfaction to help others. Perhaps the most important aspect of induction is the development of empathy. [69]

The preceding examples of induction rely in part on using the child's need to engage in approved social or moral actions and in part on the assumption that the child has a motivation toward maturity. The additional concept of empathy assumes that the child understands negative feelings others have when he has done something wrong to them, or their positive feelings following his positive acts.

Idea No. 6: It is not a good idea to use God and religion as disciplinary tools.

Many parents who are religious sometimes fall into the error of repeatedly using God or religion to back up their demands. The problem with this is that the child then sees God as the source of all these restrictions and criticisms. This certainly is not a help to either God or the Church. Learning Exercise 34.2 is a series of questions to ask yourself to better understand how your discipline. For religious parents it is important to teach about God and God's commandments for living but it is not necessary to use God as a threat or a parenting tool.

LEARNING EXPERIENCE 34.1

1 = not at all like me   **2 = somewhat like me**

3 = like me   **4 = very much like me**

1. I use (or would use) self-oriented induction in pointing out my children's consequences directly to them.

1   2   3   4

2. I I use (or would use) feeling techniques to help my children understand the consequences of their behavior for themselves and others.

1   2   3   4

3. I I feel (or would feel) that helping my children to understand and have an emotional response for their actions is important.

1   2   3   4

4. I explain (or would explain) feelings to my children because an explanation is often powerful enough to change behavior.

1   2   3   4

5. I use (or would use) feeling techniques for both negative and positive acts.

1   2   3   4

6. I want (or would want) my statements to elicit guilt or self-condemnation in my children.

1   2   3   4

7. I am (or would be) more concerned with the action rather than with judgment of the child.

1   2   3   4

8. I want (or would want) my children to feel a need to engage in approved social or moral actions.

1   2   3   4

9. I want (or would want) to help my children understand that they are individuals capable of comprehending more mature concepts.

1   2   3   4

10. I think (or would think) that induction is superior to love withdrawal or power and punishment.

1   2   3   4

LESSON EIGHT

How to Change Behavior without Force

After you have successfully completed this lesson, you should be able to do the following:

1. More effectively use reasoning with children and adolescents.

2. Describe ways to help youth acquire positive identities and the importance of doing so.

3. Change behavior using self-image dissonance.

Principle 35

You can reason with the unreasonable.

Idea No. 1: Reasoning with children must be done to develop rational human beings.

Reasoning with children is the first step to producing responsible adults. Parents help children understand the connection between cooperation and having time for fun as described in the following dialogue:

Mom: Okay kids, everybody has their job assignments. Let's get at it!

Michael: But, Mom! I don't want to help gather the laundry. It's too har Can't I feed Max instead?

Spencer: Feeding Max is one of my jobs. You can clean the bathroom f me.

Lauren: I'll set the table later, Mom. I want to go out and play.

Mom: Now, listen, kids. Without everyone's cooperation, the hou won't get cleaned and we won't be able to go to the beach. Y enjoy going to the beach, but we won't go until everyone pitch in. If Michael doesn't help with the laundry, and Lauren does set the table, and Spencer doesn't get the bathroom done, Mo will have to do it all and there won't be any time left to pl Who wants to go to the beach?

Kids: We do!!!

Parents may sometimes appeal to the child's developing sense of love and concern for parents and other family members.

An appeal to a child's own goals for academic or social success may be effective as in the following situation:

Daughter: Why can't I wear it?

Mother: Well, it is just inappropriate.

Daughter: I think it looks good and it covers my body. It's modest.

Mother: That's true; it is colorful and modest, but the style communicates a special meaning in this culture that it does not in our old culture.

Daughter: So what? I'm not that way.

Mother: Well, would you print a sign that says that and wear it around your neck?

Daughter: No.

Mother: Well, that's what I'm trying to say. I want the best for you and I'm trying to help you be a success in this culture.

Another effective method is to appeal to the child's desires for maturity and responsibility as shown below:

Mother: Did you do the job I gave you?

Child: No!

Mother: When you learn to be more responsible, people will be able to depend on you more, and it also shows me I can depend on you when I leave you in charge.

Idea No. 2: Reasoning with children and adolescents is most effective when the parent refers to the child's own goals.

Would it not be a delightful world if we could just sit down with our children and reason together? It would be wonderful if we could just talk things over instead of fighting, manipulating, bargaining, or using rewards and punishments to bring about good behavior.

Idea No. 3: The quality of reasoning we use with children is important.

Sometimes it is necessary to use a simple bit of logic that says: "Well, I'm your parent and it is my job to help you make good decisions so here is what I say." But the quality can be upgraded and expanded, as you will find when completing Learning Experience 35.1. There is no limit to the upgrade and improvement possible in learning to use our minds to solve the problems of daily living with each other. And this applies to the parent-child relationship. But the level of reasoning in the parent-child relationship will probably not be much higher than that used by the parents. Thus, the first step is to use your best quality reasoning with your children.

Idea No. 4: The quantity or amount of reasoning is important.

While there is no upper limit to the quality of reasoning, there is to the quantity but most families are not in danger of over-using reasoning. Therefore, take some time to do what is commonly called "thinking things over," or "talking things out." Rarely will children resent or be upset about going over their lives using a calm, rational, logical approach that may even be repetitive to the parent. In essence, you can't give too much time to being reasonable.

Now, answer the questions in the following Learning Experiences and learn from your answers how you can use reason to help your children.

LEARNING EXPERIENCE 35.1

Ways to Reason with the Unreasonable

Select from the list below the reasons which you might like to use sometime as a parent. The following hints may be useful:

1. Each could be an answer to the oft heard words: "Why should I?"

2. Often your reasoning may start with the word "because."

Types of Reasons and Goals to Appeal to when Reasoning with Children and Adolescents.

After each of the following statements, write your own example of reasoning with that particular justification for a request .

1. The youth's immediate happiness.

2. The child's long-term happiness.

3. The well-being of the family.

4. The necessity for obeying civil law and legitimate authority.

5. Improve feelings toward and help loved ones.

6. Because it is the way people do things in your culture.

7. Because it agrees and fits with what the child believes.

8. Because doing this will result in a better relationship with others, especially with the parent making the request.

Principle 36

Remember who you are.

My father always told my brother and me to "Remember who you are," when we were leaving the house. As we left, we would joke with each other, "Do you remember who you are?" said I, and he would answer, "No, who are you?" "I don't know," "Do you know who I am?" "No, but I'll find out and let you know." And so we would laugh and joke about this curious advice from our father. But, we always knew what he meant and the wisdom of this advice becomes more meaningful with each passing year.

Idea No. 1: It is not unusual for adolescents to try out several identities.

Most psychologists who have studied adolescence, especially Erik Erikson, point out that the primary task of adolescence is to establish an identity: to find out who they are and to develop an accurate and positive self-image. In most cases, a number of different roles or images will be tried and most will not be acceptable or work for the individual, and hence, will be cast off. Then the person will try to discover who he or she is once again.

Once an identity or self-image is accepted, even if it is only temporary, it is defended with ferocity. The establishment of a positive self-concept, then, becomes the first step in our lifestyle plan and individual day-to- day actions. For the parent, and to help the child acquire a long-term style of life, the development of an accurate and positive self-concept is the most important step. Both actions and words will influence the type of self-concept an individual acquires.

Every young adolescent is actively engaged in trying to discover who and what he is. The parent does not have to initiate this process; it is already ongoing. The strength and power of this "seeking an identity" is most clearly seen in the strict divisions between types of people who can be readily observed in junior high school and continue on through high school.

Idea No. 2: Families have identities.

This process, however, is not restricted to adolescence. At every stage of the life cycle our identities continue to be shaped. Parents go through "identity-seeking" and labels, often in search of becoming what a "good parent" means to them. Our families have identities, too. These are usually shaped by the kinds of people who make up or characterize a particular family.

Idea No. 3: The best way to help a youth find a positive, solid identity is to help him find it in the family.

Parents can help a child acquire an identity by discussing with the child how they feel, where they excel, and what they are doing. A parent points out positive attributes when he notices them, and at the same time, tries to point out that negative responses and behavior need not occur and that sometimes we all make mistakes. With encouragement and help, the child may come to see himself as good, intelligent, competent, and likeable.

When I was 16 I was totally in love with a guy for about a year, and finally we went out on a date, and after that we became good friends and were together a lot. When things were going well (I thought), he told me he didn't want to be together anymore.

I was crushed. I became really depressed. It had some effect on my family.

One night, my father came down to my room and talked with me. He told me he understood that I'd been through a difficult experience. He said that I couldn't let it affect my life so much. He told me who I was, he told me that I was a happy, carefree person. He told me that I couldn't go on being depressed.

I realized how much I was letting this experience affect my life, and the life of my family. I saw that there had to be an end, and I saw that I really was a happy person.

Idea No. 4: When it comes to establishing identities, focus on what a person is "inside" more than on their actions or behaviors.

Sometimes people display the opposite personality of who they really are, but with kind interpretations and assistance from loving and trusting parents, they will come to see that their errors and imperfections are not who they really are and they will come to see more positive aspects of themselves. At a time like this, it is best to focus on who a person IS rather than paying too much attention to his actions or behavior because young people make many mistakes and errors that should not be used to establish an identity. If their identities seem to be based on actions or behaviors, they begin to believe that they are stupid or are failures.

Self-growth is a complicated process with many facets that are continually being shaped. There is one self-image related to work, one related to school, one related to goodness, and others related to such things as intelligence and talent. Some of these firm up earlier than others. Acquiring an identity is also a two-way process between parent and teen. Not only does the parent give the teen feedback and encouragement, but the teen helps to shape the parent's "identity" of himself as a parent as well. Parents need feedback and encouragement too. Turn now to Learning Experiences 36.1.

LEARNING EXPERIENCE 36.1

How I as a Parent Might Be Rated by a Hypothetical Adolescent as Answered by an Adolescent in Your Family.

For the following questions, choose the most appropriate answer to how your imaginary or hypothetical adolescent would rate you as a parent using the rankings of *more, just right,* and *less.*

_____ 1. My parent discusses how I feel.

_____ 2. My parent points out positive attributes as well as negative responses, allowing for mistakes.

_____ 3. My parent offers encouragement and help.

_____ 4. I have a loving and trusting relationship with my parent

_____ 5. My parent focus more on who I am rather than on my actions or behavior.

The following lists are just some of the possible "identities" or labels for adolescents that can exist in the world. First, quickly add to the lists other identities you can think of for each group.

TEEN	PARENT	FAMILY
Preppies	Strict	Organized
Jocks	Easy	Close
Brains	Hard nosed	Active
Partiers	Loving	Do nothing

Principle 37

Helping a child match positive actions with a positive self-image

I have an uncle who is a doctor. He is so smart, and he's a nice person. Whenever I get good grades in my classes, my mother always tells me that I am like my smart uncle. That makes me happy and encourages me to study hard because I want to be like him.

Now consider "A Man of Your Word."

Son, I've noticed lately that you are not doing your chores, and as a result your brothers and sisters are not doing theirs, and the house is getting very dirty. Can you help me understand why not? Son, I know you are a man of your word and that if you say you will do something you have the capabilities to do it. Will you put forth the effort to do your chores from now on?

Next consider the story about a sister who doesn't gossip.

My sister doesn't like gossip. When she starts to gossip I'll just say, "Sis, you're gossiping!!" and she'll realize that she is becoming what she doesn't want to be and will stop. Or, I'll just ask her (or anyone) if they are doing what they don't believe in just to get them thinking about what they are doing.

Now after considering these three short examples, you may see the fundamentals of this new principle. It focuses on identities first and letting the behavior follow.

Idea No. 1: Behavior will change to match a person's identity.

Researchers have shown that when one's actions are not in harmony with one's beliefs, an unpleasant emotional experience is produced. This is called "dissonance" and will continue until either the actions are changed to match the self beliefs or the self beliefs are changed to match the actions. Others can help us change by using a non- confrontive direct approach by pointing out the conflict.

But, the actual change is done by examining ourselves. Now we will return to some more examples to illustrate this important principle.

Thomas, my 13-year-old son, comes home with a report card--five "Bs" and three "Cs". I realize that he is not applying himself because he has a lot of free time on his hands.

"Son, I know you're determined and unstoppable on the basketball court, yet I see you're not applying those same traits to your school work. I know you are a hard worker."

Idea No. 2: Sometimes all a parent has to do is point out to a child/adolescent what kind of person he/she is.

"It's not like you to do that." This is something that you can tell a good child or adolescent who already has a good self-identity. Maybe he/she just made a stupid mistake--they all do sometimes. Just help him realize that he made a mistake and that he really is a good person who doesn't usually do those things, and he will probably realize it and not do it next time.

Idea No. 3: Minimize mistakes and help children see that their mistakes are not them as people.

Some other words you can use to guide children:

"That doesn't sound like you."

"You know better than that."

"You're a much better person than that."

"That surprises me; you've never acted that way before."

"That's so out of character for you."

"You've always been a good sharer."

Idea No. 4: Use a good self-concept to inspire children and adults to behave better.

One of the most powerful forces influencing what humans do is self- concept. At a young age, people acquire beliefs and opinions about what kind of person they are. They hold to these beliefs tenaciously for that is their identity. It is in this area of human development that parents can give a great deal of help in two ways. First, they can help children acquire positive self-images, and then they will find that by using a little wisdom and very little power or force they can help the child act in desirable ways.

Idea No. 5: If self-image and actions do not match, most children and adults will change their actions rather than their concepts of identity.

To discover how this principle works go to Learning Experiences 37.1 and 37.2. In Learning Experience 37.2 a series of steps are given to help you put this principle of self-image dissonance into action.

LEARNING EXPERIENCE 37.1

Discovering the Principles of Self-Change

1.　Have you found that most people, even at a young age, have an identity or a belief about what kind of person they are?

2.　If a person acts in a way that is not in agreement with the kind of person they think they are, what will happen? Choose one of the following:

　　c.　They will change what they are doing when they realize that it does not fit with their self-image.

　　b.　They will change their self-image to agree with their actions.

In reality, either of the above could happen, but our self-images are usually stronger than the actions. Children then will change their behavior to agree with who and what they think they are. What does this imply for a parent who wants to teach his or her child to be moral? Write your answer below

LEARNING EXPERIENCE 37.2

Helping Children Match Behavior to a Positive Self-Image

Choose one of the following and then write what you would say and do with your children. Be very specific about the situation and what you would say and do and why or give an example of when someone close to you has done one of the six things listed below to guide a child toward positive behavior.

1.   Help the child to establish an identity or self-concept before a specific behavior is likely to occur.

2.   Help the child see the conflict between what he is doing and the self-image you desire him to have.

3.   Put the child in a situation where there is the best chance the child will act in a way that is in agreement with the desired self-concept.

4.   Treat the child as if he already possesses the desired trait even if it exists only at a low level.

5.   Help the child dress and engage in activities that reflect the belief that the child has the desired quality.

6.   Tell the child that he resembles or reminds you of someone who has that desired characteristic.

SUMMARY

Instructions: Mark *a* if the statement is true and *b* if it is false. Submit to Instructor.

1.   It is better to use only consequences with children and delay reasoning until the child reaches adolescence.

2.   It is the quality of reasoning which is important not the quantity.

3.   The three kinds of reasoning that can be applied to children are to appeal to the child's immediate happiness, the child's long-term happiness, and the well-being of the family.

4.   It is common for adolescents to try out several identities.

5.   The best way to help a youth find a positive, solid identity is to help him find it with the school or with peers.

6.   Young people change their identities to match their behavior, but not their behavior to match their identities.

7.   A positive self-concept is related to identity and can influence behavior.

8.   It is better to establish a self-concept before a specific behavior is likely to occur.

9.   A parent should never point out a conflict between what a child is doing and the child's self-image.

10. It is good to treat the child as if he already possesses the desired trait even it exists at a low level.

LESSON NINE

How to Improve Communication

After you have successfully completed this lesson, you should be able to do the following:

1. Develop skills in solving family problems using the "no lose" method.

2. Improve communication skills.

Principle 38

Use "no-lose" problem-solving methods

Idea No. 1: There are many good problem-solving methods for handling family problems.

In our home we used to have quite a bit of fighting. A fight would start over the silliest ting and continue until Mom got involved (or until they would come running to me yelling their complaints, "Dad, Spencer hit. . . .") For awhile I tried letting them settle their own differences. I told them that if I had to interfere, no one would be pleased with the outcome. Still problems occurred, and I felt like I was constantly playing the judge.

We decided to incorporate the idea mentioned. Instead of running to Mom and Dad with the complaint, they had to go to the refrigerator and write on a piece of paper, the date, their name (the plaintiff), and the defendant's name. Then, they would write a brief explanation of what happened. (I essentially ignored any complaints.)

On Sundays, we held family court. (Often the kids would forget what they had been fighting over.) So far, not interfering and ignoring their complaints has dropped the incidence of fighting in our home. The complaint sheet has gotten smaller over the weeks, too. Rewarding frequently the times they get along also encourages good behavior.

This is just one of many ways to use family problem-solving methods.

Idea No. 2: Family councils allow children to take part in setting up rules and punishments.

Another effective problem-solving method is holding a family council as described in the following story:

Family councils were usually the place where new rules were implemented. My dad would usually start off by congratulating us on what wonderful jobs we were doing in the family. He would then mention an area-not cleaning bedrooms, not putting dishes away, tying up the phone lines forever, etc.—that had given him concern lately and wondered what we thought we could do to correct the situation. Generally, we were already aware of the problem and were willing to find a solution. However, there were those times when the kids in my family didn't feel the same way about a problem that my dad felt, and rules had to be imposed if order was to be maintained. Furthermore, consequences for breaking the rule were discussed at the same time the rule was implemented. That way, all of us were sure what was going to happen if we chose to break a rule.

I found that I was a lot more careful about breaking rules when I knew the punishment ahead of time. I also liked the fact that the consequences usually fit the crime. If someone didn't do their dishes, they did the family's dishes for a week. If curfew was broken, they had to subtract the time they were late from their curfew the next time they went out. If I left my clothes on my bedroom floor, my mom would pick them up for me and I would have to pay to get them back.

I never felt cheated or abused when I was punished. I had generally helped to decide on the consequences. I also feel that my parents were relatively flexible with changing the rules to fit the needs of the individual children. When 12:00 curfews became a little too early for the older teenagers, it was extended, etc. I feel that because my parents were so fair in letting us help establish the rules and consequences in our family, there were no serious infractions. The most my parents ever needed to do was hold a family council and remind us what the family rules were.

Idea No. 3: Using a "No Lose" approach is a very simple way to solve many conflicts.

Another effective problem-solving method is the "win-win" or "no lose" method. Both the parent and the adolescent win because the solution of the conflict must be acceptable to both parties. Using this method, both parent and adolescent send messages and use listening in communicating about the problem. They work at the problem until they obtain a solution which is acceptable to both. The "win-win" or "no lose" method generally includes the steps found in Table 38.1.

TABLE 38.1

1. Identify and define the conflict.

2. Generate possible alternative solutions. It is important to avoid deciding which is the best solution, but instead try to think of as many solutions as possible through brainstorming.

3. Evaluate the alternative solutions together.

4. Decide together which is the best solution or the most acceptable solution.

5. Work out together a way to implement the solution--how it can be put into practice.

6. Evaluate together how the chosen solution is working and change it when one of the participants feels it isn't working.

Idea No. 4: Effective problem-solving works best when parent and child solve problems together.

Learning Experience 38.1 was designed to help see the value of using a problem-solving approach in the family. After completing it, move to Learning Experiences 38.2 to practice using the method.

LEARNING EXPERIENCE 38.1

Involving Everyone in Solutions to Family Problems

Long-lasting solutions to meet every family member's needs are necessary or the problems will return. A family problem is not solved if even one member doesn't like the solution. Some family leaders just naturally seem to bring about harmonious solutions. The purpose of this activity is to help you discover the secret of such leaders. Answering the following questions will help you determine the secrets of effective family leadership.

1. When faced with anger and pressed for an immediate solution, are effective family leaders prone to delay their reactions and take more time?

2. Do effective family leaders ask for solutions, and how many will they listen to without becoming angry themselves?

3. Do effective family leaders offer only one solution and stick to it, or do they usually consider other recommendations when theirs are rejected?

4. Do effective family leaders consider all possibilities with respect?

5. Are they willing to try out some questionable and weak solutions on a temporary basis?

6. When a solution to a problem doesn't work out as expected, do they blame and criticize others?

LEARNING EXPERIENCE 38.2

A Problem-Solving Practice

On this page use the four steps identified in this chapter to solve the following problem. Write out a conversation and identify where each step is introduced by underlining and labeling.

Father wants to watch news on TV at 5 p.m. Mother wants dinner at 5 p.m. and the children's favorite sitcom shows at 5 p.m.

All family members disagree about a proposed vacation.

Principle 39

Communication with children is about listening—not talking.

"She talks endlessly to her friends on the phone, but she just tunes me out. I just can't reach her."

"My children don't listen to anything I say." "If only we could communicate."

Idea No. 1: Communication with children is listening—not talking.

That many parents struggle with communication with their children is evidenced by these common complaints voiced by parents. A satisfying relationship with your children requires communication. To make it easier for your children to communicate with you, your communication must convince your children that you care enough to listen. Unfortunately, much of parent-child communication is one-way "talking to" in the form of nagging, reminding, criticizing, threatening, lecturing, etc. Guiding the child is necessary, but the parent must also learn to listen to the child. How does anyone know if the things being taught are making a difference without feedback? Parents should treat their children with as much consideration as they treat their friends, and that includes listening patiently to ideas and concerns they may not agree with.

Successful communication seems easy for some and elusive for others. Communication has two parts: a sending part and a receiving part. The key to success is to remember that the receiving part is most important. Communication with children is less about talking and more about *listening*. The challenge of parent-child communication is to encourage children to talk to you. Young children talk almost incessantly to their parents, but older children sometimes communicate little with their parents. Parents need to let older children know that they care enough to listen

Idea No. 2: Pay attention to the purpose of your children's communication, but ignore the style.

To be a good listener, a parent should pay attention to the *purpose* communication. Children and adolescents may not clearly indicate the purposes of their communication as shown below:

Brad: I can't stand school anymore. I'm going crazy!

Susan: I agree. If school doesn't end soon, I'll commit suicide.

George: You never trust me. I come home two hours late, and you act like I've committed a major crime. Well, I'm sick of you treating me like a baby. I hate you!

Adolescents sometimes say things they really don't mean, and unless we try to understand the purpose of their communications, we may overreact and become defensive. Parents should consider the framework or context in which the message was sent.

Parents should also avoid rejecting what our children are saying because the grammar may be incorrect or the style may be rough, such as "Give me five." Communication often means ignoring the way the message is transmitted in order to focus on the context.

Idea No. 3: Make parent-child communication a priority and plan ahead for one-on-one.

Listening to a child is a way to show love and respect. It is important to listen with a kind heart and try to *feel* as well as understand what the child is saying. In order to truly listen it is important to regard the child's view as important as one's own. To patiently listen but then ignore or disregard the child's views does not invite future conversation. Regarding the child's views means also not criticizing or judging immediately. A parent who wants communication with a child will truly consider the child's point of view even if the eventual decision is made contrary to the child's views.

Also, good communication takes time. Often it is best that talking times be one-on-one and not interrupted. Good discussions may also take place while you are working together on dishes or laundry or while you are transporting the child to school or extra-curricular activities. Parent-child communication needs to be a priority and planned ahead.

Idea No. 4: *Clarification* **and** *rephrasing* **are effective ways of learning if we understand what our children are telling us.**

Another way to improve understanding in communication is to ask for clarification. "Would you explain that to me again?" Or rephrase what you hear and respond by saying, "You think I am not being reasonable in requiring you to be home by 10:30 p.m. on week nights." Parent- child communication can be greatly improved if we really understand what the child is trying to tell us.

Learning Experience 39.1 will, as in the last chapter, help you review the main concepts of this principle.

LEARNING EXPERIENCE 39.1

Listening to Communicate

For each of the statements below indicate your level of agreement by circling the appropriate response. (**ANSWER KEY: SA=Strongly Agree; A=Agree; NS=Not Sure; D=Disagree; SD=Strongly Disagree**)

1. Parent-child communication requires the child to "shut up and listen."

SA   A   NS   D   SD

2. In communicating with children the receiving part is more important than the sending part.

SA   A   NS   D   SD

3. Parent-child communication is mostly limited by the young child's ability to talk.

SA   A   NS   D   SD

4. Communication with children requires "mutual respect" and an environment which allows them to express beliefs and feelings openly.

SA   A   NS   D   SD

5. The purpose of a child's communication may not be obvious from the words spoken.

SA   A   NS   D   SD

6. In order to encourage open communication, it may be important to ignore grammar or slang, etc.

SA   A   NS   D   SD

7. Asking for clarification is useful for understanding the message of a communication.

SA   A   NS   D   SD

Principle 40

Good communication is based on sharing and trust.

Idea No. 1: Communicate with your child by sharing your own experiences.

I knew my son was upset because he had not done as well as he wanted on a school project and in a musical program for which he had to play an instrument. I found an occasion to talk about how miserable I had been when I got a bad grade, feeling down on myself, but I had finally accepted the fact that I could not always be perfect. I told him that he probably got some of his perfectionism from me, and I told him that I hoped he would be able to deal with mistakes better than I had. My son listened with interest and afterward said, "Thanks, Mom, that was a real help!"

The above example illustrates the importance of sharing your experiences with your son or daughter to improve communication.

Idea No. 2: Good parent-child communication is based on trust.

Another key for communication is to expand the trust limits. Trust brings an added dimension of love and makes open communication more likely to happen. Trust elicits trust, and trust makes the young person more likely to trust his parents.

When I was a youth I played on the high school basketball team in a small town in Wyoming. One night a few of the other basketball players got into some trouble. Later my father said to me, "It's sad that this happened. I know if you had been there you would never have allowed such a thing to occur." This trust my father showed me expanded my feeling of trust and made it suddenly easier to talk to my father about matters that demanded trust.

Idea No. 3: A calm, problem-solving approach is needed in emotional disputes.

A third basic is that parents can take a problem-solving approach and avoid excessive emotionality with children as illustrated by the following story:

When I was a teenager I told my parents that I didn't want to take seminary that year. I expected them to get emotional and argue with me, but they did not. They sat down and discussed the problem with me. Together we looked at the pros and cons, the various options available, and we discussed which options made the most sense. Because of this experience, I learned that my parents could help me solve problems, so I felt safe telling them about my problems.

Idea No. 4: Help children understand the point of view of other person.

A fourth basic for communication in the family is to help children understand the other person's point of view.

Idea No. 5: Communicate with the child when he is ready.

Idea No. 6: Use reflective communication by listening and then responding with what you heard expressed.

A sixth basic is to not only try to understand what your child is saying but also communicate that understanding back to him/her. This task is called reflective communication and requires two basic skills as follows: 1) listening to your child's thoughts and feelings; 2) making responses that reflect the thoughts and feelings you heard your child express. Following is an example of reflective communication:

Tim: I hate algebra. It's so dumb. I wish I didn't have to take it.

Mom: You really don't like that class much do you?

Tim: I don't. But I guess I better do that dumb old homework anyway.

All his mother did was express that she understood him. Often, that is all that is needed.

Now go to Learning Experience 40.1 and review this principle by indicating your level of agreement with the main points.

LEARNING EXPERIENCE 40.1

Self-Evaluation on Communication Basics

Circle the answer the indicates how much you agree with each of the following statements. (**ANSWER KEY: SA=Strongly Agree; A=Agree; NS=Not Sure; D=Disagree; SD=Strongly Disagree**)

1. Sharing your own childhood experiences is effective in helping children through difficult times.

   SA   A   NS   D   SD

2. When I show by my words and actions that I trust my children they are more likely to communicate with me openly.

   SA   A   NS   D   SD

3. When I sit down with my child and talk calmly about the pros and cons of various actions we are better able to solve problems.

   SA   A   NS   D   SD

4. Children's arguments sometimes disappear if they can understand the other person's point of view.

   SA   A   NS   D   SD

5. It is more effective to communicate with a child when he/she is ready, so I look for teaching moments when he/she wants to talk.

   SA   A   NS   D   SD

6. Communication with my children is better when they feel that I understand them.

   SA   A   NS   D   SD

Principle 41

Communication is improved with knowing your child's world.

Idea No. 1: Communication can be increased by knowing and being involved with your children's friends.

Growing up, I can remember a house full of kids. Not only my brother and five sisters but a lot of our friends as well. Other people's kids seemed to feel right at home in my house. At least they did during the day when it was just my mom at home. My dad wasn't very good at making friends with kids our age.

I can remember several of our friends calling my mom "Mom." She seemed to have a way of making them all feel special. When kids would call, she would talk to them awhile before handing the phone to us. There were always extra mouths to feed at "after school snack time" and quite often they would still be there for morning family prayer.

My mom still has the gift of making friends with her children's friends. She especially likes my husband.

Having a mom that was friends with my friends made it a lot easier growing up, especially as a teenager. Because she knew who everyone was and what they were like, it was easy to be open with her about most of the things we would do.

Idea No. 2: Getting to know children's friends makes parenting even more fun.

Parents who know their children's friends, have them at their home, and enjoy parenting are more likely to have better communication with their children.   But communication with children involves setting up the environment for communication in many other ways besides knowing their world of friends. It also helps to be acquainted with the adolescent's world of music, movies, and styles—if for no reason other than dissuading your child from participation in some of them.

Idea No. 3: Set the stage for communication. Right after school is an optimal time for parent-child communication.

In setting the stage for communication it is important to have sufficient time, but it is also desirable to have something good to eat or drink during conversations. The age-old picture of children coming home from school and getting a snack of freshly-baked cookies or bread did more than feed children. It provided parents and children a great way to communicate about the day's activities. In fact, some scholars now claim that it is right after school when children are willing to talk about their day at school including any problems that arose there—not hours later when the parents get home from work.

Idea No. 4: Meet children's needs for privacy, humor, confidentiality, and available times for talking.

Other suggestions for setting the stage include finding a place that is private, beginning with some friendly questions, and being willing to laugh and joke around as well as be serious. It is also important to keep the information personal and to be willing to talk when the children are available. With adolescents, late night talks are effective times for communication.

LEARNING EXPERIENCE 41.1

Improving Communication with Children

Families must work and pull together. The first step to better communication with each other is to increase both understanding and cooperation. Because we are human beings, we have great skills in talking, but so often we don't do our best communicating in the family. We know how but still need to identify where to improve. The following questions are meant to help you do that.

Place an "X" in front of each statement that describes what you believe to be true or desirable.

_____1. I would like to regard his/her views as important as my own.

_____2. I would like to believe that listening is a way I can show love and respect.

_____3. I would like to listen with a kind heart, believing it is most important to feel what my child is saying.

_____4. When listening, I would like to try my best to not criticize or judge.

_____5. Sometimes I just listen and either agree or decide not to talk anymore than I have to.

_____6. I would like to control my impulse to set things straight when I am unfairly criticized.

_____7. I would like to organize my life so I have enough time to talk one-on-one.

_____8. Sometimes I could provide something good to eat or drink during conversations.

_____9. I would like to think of some friendly questions with which to open or begin our talks.

SUMMARY

Instructions: Mark *a* if the statement is true and *b* if it is false.

1. Good communication with children involves first, learning to talk on their level and second, developing a style of communicating.

2. With young children who are not skilled in communication it is important to ask for clarification and rephrasing.

3. To improve communication with children you should share your own experience, be trustworthy, and avoid excessive emotionality.

4. It is especially important to use a calm, problem-solving approach in emotional disputes.

5. It is not when you talk to a child, but how you talk to a child that is important.

6. Communication is unrelated to knowing and being involved with your child's friends.

7. Right after school is an optimal time for parent-child communication, but late at night is not.

8. It is better to remain serious and responsible rather than laughing and joking in communication with children and adolescents.

9. In the "win-win" or "no-lose" method of resolving conflicts, the leader of the family decides what is best and carefully explains the proposed solution, listens to the family's input, and then voting.

10. The "win-win" or "no-lose" method should be used instead of family councils and parental leadership.

LESSON TEN

Tips on Being an Example

After you have successfully completed this lesson, you should be able to do the following:

1. Describe the powerful influence of modeling on children's behavior.

2. Outline seven reasons why modeling works.

3. Increase the effectiveness of a model.

Principle 42

Children read their examples more than their books.

When I was a little girl, playing house was my absolute favorite pastime. Because of this, I thought my mom had the coolest job in the world—a housewife. I would spend hours carefully watching every move she made and would mimic her actions in my little playhouse in the back yard. I guess my mom was pretty smart and caught on to what I was doing when she saw me, her four-year-old, pretending to vacuum, then carry on a conversation at the same time. Instead of sitting me in front of the TV while she tried to clean the house, she invited me to come along and help. [Now this young mother's example is instructive.]

Idea No. 1: Setting an example by living the principles you want your children to emulate is the most subtle and yet the most powerful tool in shaping your child.

Now here is an example of a father who was a positive role model:

My best friend, Clint, was just telling me about his favorite role model, his father, who recently passed away of cancer. When he was a boy, his dad would take the time to make Clint feel important. While finishing their basement, Clint's father took the extra time to put up a replica piece of sheetrock and with a pencil drew where the nails needed to go. Then, side by side, they hammered away to get the job done.

Clint says those experiences have given him confidence in himself. He wanted to be just like his dad. Many people have since commented on how much Clint looks like his father and has his same mannerisms which he takes as the highest compliment imaginable.

Idea No. 2: Parents can strive to be more positive and effective role models.

Sometimes the model is not a parent but a parent's goals are benefited just the same as demonstrated by the following words of a Korean student:

I would like to be a person who was admired and respected by people. For example, when I was about 8 years old, President Park was the most admired and respected person in Korea because he was the one who rebuilt the Korean economic system and set up a new political system after the Korean War. I really wanted to be like him, so I read his biography and tried to imitate what he had done in elementary school.

Everyone knows that children imitate and copy adults, but children also copy some people more than others. According to modeling theory as discussed by Bandura,[68] children are more likely to copy others who are powerful, important, warm and loving, respected and admired, competent or significant in their own lives. Most parents are not going to become powerful, but they can be warm and loving and take a significant, even powerful role in their children's lives.

Idea No. 3: Parents can provide positive role models through books and associations with other adults who model desired behaviors.

Parents can also influence how much their children copy other adults and which adults they copy and they can encourage their children to read good books which portray worthy models. Parents can be very selective concerning the role models their children observe on TV programs and in movies. They can encourage association with relatives and neighbors who model desired positive behaviors. Parents can also arrange for their children and adolescents to participate in activities led by youth leaders whose personal lives portray the desired positive behaviors.

In spite of pervasive negative influences in many cultures, there is still much good modeled in almost any culture—in literature, in films and plays, and also in our families. Concerned parents need to actively model positive behaviors themselves and facilitate modeling of other adults worthy of emulation. Now go to Learning Experiences 42.1 and 42.2.

LEARNING EXPERIENCE 42.1

Understanding How Children Copy Role Models

This activity will help you understand why children copy some role models more than others, and under what circumstances more modeling takes place. Answering these questions will help you understand better the factors that affect the amount of modeling or copying that takes place and what parents can do to increase (or decrease) the amount of copying that takes place. Think about your life and any experiences when you copied the behaviors of an adult. Then, answer the following questions:

1. Were you more likely to imitate a person who was successful in getting rewards?

2. Were you more likely to identify with a person who was warm and loving?

3. Were you more likely to want to be like a person who was respected and admired?

4. Were you more likely to copy a competent person?

5. Were you more likely to identify with and copy persons who pointed out similarities between you and themselves?

6. Would you have continued following the example of a person if you received no rewards when you did what he/she did?

7. Did it help when the persons who you wanted to copy explained with words how and why to act the way they did?

8. Did your parents ever help you be around or close to a positive role model that you admired?

9. Did it help when a role model set an example that was not too hard to follow but was within your ability to copy?

10. Did your parents ever help you to find good examples in the books you read, the stories you heard, or the television or movies you watched?

Principle 43

An example reminds a child of what is right.

A major rule in my home stated that shoes were not to be worn in the house. A violation would bring severe discomfort to my behind. Growing up, I was always reminded by the example of my parents that shoes were to be left at the door. When I would come home alone, my parents shoes were sitting by the doorway, reminding me to take off my shoes before entering.

Models work for many reasons. Sometimes they remind the child of internalized social rules such as giving, charity, or helping others in distress. Having previously learned these rules, a child may need only be reminded of them in order to willingly comply. Under normal circumstances both adults and children often need to be reminded of proper behavior. For example, in one large family with young children, the mother faced the typical problem of having her children just drop what they carried into the house. Upon entering the front door, coats, instead of being hung up, were simply pitched on the couch or chair. Soon the entryway was piled with books, sacks, and coats.

To eliminate this problem, the mother asked her husband to model what should be done. He acted out his part with excellence; upon entering the house he would say aloud, "I'd better hang up my coat and take this sack into the kitchen." He kept this up for a few weeks and soon, with the help of a few discussions, the children just accepted the idea that items were to be put away.

Idea No. 1: Parents who model proper behavior help children learn proper behavior.

This same family used a similar approach to model courtesy when talking to each other. To halt disrespect and anger in conversation, the parents resolved to model respect for one another and a positive attitude for their children. They found that this, in conjunction with verbally stating their expectations, immediately improved the quality of language and attitudes in the home.

Idea No. 2: Models reveal socially acceptable rewards.

The other night I was visiting my girlfriend when her married sister and brother-in-law dropped in with their cute little one-and-a-half-year-old named Ashley. Everyone was delighted because playing with Ashley is considered to be a rare treat. As I watched each person interact with Ashley, I noticed how often Ashley was expected to model certain behaviors—of course, under the unspoken rule that if she would imitate certain behaviors, she would be showered with love and affection (and sometimes even candy) for her responsiveness. I watched Ryan, her 11-year-old uncle, teach her how to fall to the ground whenever she was shot by an imaginary pistol. I watched Grandma show her how to give "loves" and kisses, and then expect "loves" and kisses in return.

Finally, the ritual of saying goodbye was something to behold. First, Ashley was expected go give everyone "loves" after which she was prodded to wink. After winking, they would have Ashley "show her teeth" by opening her mouth wide. Last of all, Ashley was expected to wave her hand in the air and say "Bye" while everyone else mimicked this behavior. I realize now more fully how children are taught through modeling and then rewarded when they imitate properly.

This view depicts the child's active effort to seek rewards through the model. Rewards, or reinforcements, can be verbal "pats on the back" or material rewards such as money.

Idea No. 3: A model increases social pressure.

In one family a child was exceptionally negative about life. She didn't like her food, the games other children played, activities or shows her friends participated in or saw, etc. The parents handled this problem by acting before the negative child would bring up criticism. They quickly asked another child a question that the parent knew would be answered positively. For instance, "How do you like the salad tonight?" "Did you have fun while we were gone?" "Are the kids at school nice?"

Over the weeks, it soon became clear to her that the negative attitudes she held were clearly out of line with all her brothers and sisters. She finally started to be more positive. In a non-forceful way the modeling of other family members effectively exerted a pressure or demand on her to be more positive.

Idea No. 4: A model shows ways to relieve distress.

How do you feel about seeing a dog straining at a leash, or a blind person trying to put a coin in a vending machine? Most of us can imagine how we would feel in similar circumstances, causing distress or discomfort. To relieve that distress, we can ignore the matter, quickly forget it, or rationalize it away. Occasionally, however, we might obtain relief by aiding the person (or animal) in need of help. By relieving their distress, we relieve our own. Many acts of kindness no doubt result from such feelings. The role of a model in facilitating this type of response is to provide examples of acts which the observer comes to recognize as relieving distress for both the distressed party and the observer. For instance, suppose a preschool boy sees a girl fall from her chair and hurt herself. Will the boy act by trying to comfort the girl who fell, or by trying to clean any scratches? Perhaps on this occasion, an adult (model) appears and proceeds to comfort the hurt child, whereupon she ceases crying and begins to smile. After seeing this, the boy will probably also be relieved and will come to associate the modeled behavior with relief of his own distress. In future instances, he will have a tool at his disposal for relieving uncomfortable feelings he experiences when seeing another person hurt.

For almost any emotional distress we depend on models to learn how to react. Whenever my family would go to friends' houses, I was never sure what to expect; and I was always afraid that I wouldn't fit in with everyone else. To relieve this stress, I would just watch my parents, and then act in ways they did; or, if other children were there, I would follow their examples. By doing this I felt like I fit in.

Idea No. 5: A model is an example of desirable or understandable behavior.

This explanation assumes a desire in adults and children to do the correct thing. Usually, as a person matures, he becomes more aware of community rules and conventions, which prescribe what is proper. How often, for example, does one call up and ask his/her friend what he is "wearing" tonight, or look around at what others (models) are wearing as a confirmation of what is appropriate attire?

The younger a person is, the fewer rules he knows and understands, and the more he needs a mature example as a model. Allowing the child to witness acts is a necessary prescription for teaching in these cases. Sometimes, a mere expression of a rule may be sufficient. "When sister cries, comfort her." More often, however, such verbal exhortations and expressions alone will not be enough. Children, as well as adults, quickly forget the meaning of such platitudes. What is needed is the opportunity to observe what is advocated. Although children may be motivated to do the right thing, unless they have the chance to actually mimic, duplicate, or emulate the behavioral implications of rules they learn, they may remain unable to do what is appropriate.

Idea No. 6: A model can demonstrate self-rewards.

In our family I have grown up getting basically good grades. My younger brother, John, could see this. John began to see how much easier things were for me as a result of getting good grades. I was happier and more content with my studies as well as my position in the home. Seeing the self-reward I was getting, I imagine this impressed upon John that he might be a happier person by getting good grades.

Adult models often pattern behavior that is self-reinforcing. A mother may give to a charity and afterwards smile and say how good that made her feel. A child picks up on these consequences and will then emulate the behavior as long as it makes him feel good also. If it does not make him feel good, he will stop.

As mentioned before, one can regard verbal exhortations to share toys, for instance, as noneffective because the child, if he has the view discussed above, will not feel good letting someone else share what he wants for himself. Only if the child sees that the adult is happy about sharing will such self-sacrificing behavior bring joy to the child. Modeling is therefore a way to prime the child r pleasant emotional experiences when acting in an altruistic manner. Once acquired, the altruistic act will be repeated as long as the person can give himself a pat on the back for doing it.

Idea No. 7: A natural desire to imitate exists.

My son is almost two years old, and although he has entered a stage where he wants to be independent and in control, part of this means wanting to do what his parents do. Right now he refuses to sit in a high chair because he wants to be in a big chair like Mommy and Daddy. He won't let us put his bib on unless we put our "bibs" (aprons) on. He has to have the same things we eat, use the napkins when we do, etc. It seems as though he is always saying things like "Mommy's shirt.. . .

Perry's shirt." It is very important to him right now that he can do what we do. In fact, when he goes to bed at night, he tries to make sure I will be going to bed too. It's a lot of fun, but also a pain sometimes.

We have saved this explanation until last, as it may be the most refreshing way to view the effects of modeling. Simply stated, children emulate parents because they like to imitate. It is a natural response, maybe even genetically programmed. A psychobiologist would suggest that infants and children imitate because imitative behavior was selectively adaptive, in an evolutionary sense, to the preservation of the species. Children parrot their peers and echo their parents, often being referred to as "chips off the old block." When we look at children, we often look at mirrors of parental behaviors. As they mature, some of these attributes stick and become part of their own personality.

Principle 44

It is possible to increase the effectiveness of a model.

At the preschool where I teach, we reward the children for certain behaviors by giving them stickers—the scratch and sniff kind. We put them on the back of the child's hand or on a certain piece of work. As a child receives a sticker, we encourage all other children to behave as so- and-so did so they can get a sticker, too. We, as teachers, try to be the models for the children and hence they receive rewards for doing as we ask. One example of this is working quietly and carefully during activity time. The children are allowed to choose a game or activity, work with it, and then return it neatly to the shelf. A child who does especially well will receive a sticker, and therefore acts as a model. This technique has worked very well for us.

Ideas No. 1 and 2: Modeling can be increased by rewarding the model and then rewarding the children for copying the model.

The emotional expressions of models receiving rewards produce similar emotions in children. Models who receive praise and admiration tend to be attributed prestige, status, and competence, which in turn influence imitation by children. From this we learn some steps to be taken which increase the effectiveness of the model.

1. Reward the model.

2. Reward the children for copying the model.

3. Use language with modeling.

4. Provide opportunity for practice or rehearsal.

5. Build new behaviors on old behaviors.

6. Provide other models.

7. Be competent and powerful.

8. Be warm and loving.

9. Be prestigious.

10. Be similar.

Idea No. 3: Provide opportunity for practice or rehearsal.

Imitation can be enhanced through overt practice or rehearsal. This principle is used by coaches of some sports, finding that learning a skill is enhanced by showing films and asking athletes to imagine themselves performing the skill.

Idea No. 5: Build new behaviors on old behaviors.

Modeling outcomes are best achieved when they use previously learned behaviors. For example, sharing of candy will occur best when the child's ability to communicate, divide portions, and empathize are already established. Even on occasions when children attend closely, reproduction of an adult's behavior may be deficient because required components of the behavioral pattern are lacking.

Idea No. 6: Provide other models.

Peers often replace parental figures as principal models and agents of socialization. The process becomes more complicated under conditions in which children are exposed to parental and peer models who display conflicting standards. However, the selection of peer models is greatly influenced by values prevailing in the home. Children tend to choose friends who share similar values and who are, therefore, more likely to reinforce familiar standards of conduct than to serve as sources of conflict. In addition, parents can help their children find good role models.

Idea No. 7: Be competent and powerful. Idea No. 8: Be warm and loving.

A warm and loving adult elicits considerably more imitative behavior than a model who lacks these qualities. . However, these characteristics may be only facilitating and not necessary conditions for imitation. Children who had a highly nurturing adult model were more inclined to accept low standards set by the model than high standards or expectations. Thus, the conclusion that adult nurturing facilitates modeling may be true only under some conditions.

Idea No. 9: Be prestigious.

Imitation is influenced not only by immediate consequences to the model, but also by distinctive status symbols, e.g., prestige, power, competence, socioeconomic status, etc. Models who are experts, or celebrities, are imitated more. The effect of this prestige carries over from one area to another, as imitative responses even generalize to unfamiliar persons if they are similar to past reward-producing models.

Idea No. 10: Be similar.

A model's prestigious qualities may not only increase the probability of imitative behavior, but also produce stable value changes. This is demonstrated in the following story by a young girl very much influenced by the accomplishments of her father.

Because my dad is a very successful and competent person in his business, I believe I have tried to model some of his behaviors, particularly his trait of being generous. I've seen him pay for others' dinners, treat people to things, give gifts, and take time out to listen to others. Consequently, I try to do the same. It comes naturally now but as I grew up it seemed that I'd do things because I saw my dad do them.

Persons told they have qualities in common with a model are more inclined to imitate responses portrayed by the model than subjects who initially share no common characteristics. The mother who says, "You're lazy just like your dad," is unwittingly likely to increase the child's laziness.

LEARNING EXPERIENCE 44.1

Increasing the Effectiveness of Learning from Models

The ten steps to increase the effectiveness of a model are listed in the table below. Describe what you would do to help children learn from you as a role model. Discuss these with a partner or group and then fill in the blanks.

STEPS	WHAT I WOULD DO

1. Reward the model

2. Reward children for copying the model

3. Use language with modeling

4. Provide opportunity for practice or rehearsal

5. Building new behaviors on old behaviors

6. Provide other models

7. Be competent and powerful

8. Be warm and loving

9. Be prestigious

10. Be similar

SUMMARY

Instructions: Mark *a* if the statement is true and *b* if it is false. Submit to Instructor.

1. Setting an example by living the principles you want your children to emulate is the most subtle and yet most powerful tool in shaping your child.

2. When the parents do not set a good example there is no way to provide modeling for children.

3. If your children do not copy or model you, it may be because of your personality and there is nothing you can do.

4. Modeling works because modeling reveals acceptable rewards, lower social pressure, and shows ways to relieve distress.

5. Modeling works well and is independent of using rewards.

6. You have to teach children to copy and imitate.

7. There are at least ten practical steps that can be used to increase the effectiveness of a model.

8. A mother who says "You're lazy just like your Dad" is likely to help the child overcome laziness.

9. Prestigious models or those who have prestige, power, and competence are more likely to be imitated.

10. If one is a good model, it is unnecessary and sometimes even harmful to explain the modeled behavior.

LESSON ELEVEN

Moving towards a Better Family Life

After you have successfully completed this lesson, you should be able to do the following:

1. Use rational confrontation when teaching responsibility.

2. Recognize the strong influence of television on behavior and learn how to counteract television's negative effects.

3. Address the issue of fighting in the family and realize the value of stopping fighting entirely.

Principle 45

Jimmy must have had a long day in Ms. Carson's first-grade classroom. At any rate the teacher's repeated reminders to be quiet were to no avail. In desperation she sent him out.

I was the student teacher of the classroom and was asked to check on Jimmy. He was sitting on a bench with his chin resting on his hand as I sat down beside him.

"Jimmy, do you know why you're here?"

"Yes."

"Can you tell me?"

"I wasn't quiet."

"That's right, and it was disrupting to the class, wasn't it?"

"Yes."

"Well, what can we do about it?"

"Be quiet, I guess."

"Can you do that?" "Yes."

"Great, Jimmy. Let's shake on it."

We shook. Jimmy smiled and was great the rest of the day. Periodically I remembered to pass by him and whisper encouragement and compliments on his improved conduct.

Rational confrontation teaches responsibility.

This successful confrontation was reported by a student when completing her student teaching experience in a small rural school. Consider the next illustration:

The above examples outlines an approach recommended by William Glasser, 70 who has proposed a practical way to deal with children using rational confrontation, which he calls "reality therapy." While Glasser has proposed an entire approach to therapy, we have selected the heart of his program to illustrate how direct confrontation can be used to influence children's future behavior.

Idea No. 1: The misbehaving child must make a value judgment about misbehavior if the child is to improve.

The object of a confrontation is to help a child make a value judgment about his or her behavior and a commitment to improve. Glasser 71 asks parents to first confront the child with his or her behavior and ask if that behavior is going to be satisfying or not.

Idea No. 2: The misbehaving child must identify future results of behaviors.

The parent then asks the child to identify future results of this behavior and asks if it is going to be satisfying to the child or to others. This rational approach of pointing out consequences and having the child evaluate those consequences helps bring him or her to the point of accepting responsibility.

Idea No. 3: The child must make better plans for future behavior.

After present behavior is examined in terms of consequences, a child is given the opportunity to formulate several alternative plans of behavior to bring about more desirable results; a decision is then made as to which is the best plan of action to follow.

Idea No. 4: The child must make a commitment and stay with it.

If a child makes a responsible decision, Glasser then asks the child to make a commitment. He maintains that commitment is essential for the development of maturity and feelings of self-worth, eventually leading to a stable self-identity.

Parents should accept no excuses for not following through once a commitment is made; previously decided-upon consequences need to follow if the commitment is not upheld. A child will then learn to recognize his or her own responsibility for actions taken, including assuming the consequences of misbehavior. Glasser assures parents that if they exact these standards, they will not alienate their children from them. Instead, as children successfully comply with or meet these standards, they will gain in self-respect, closeness, and love for their parents.

Idea No. 5: Freedom to choose is vital for reality therapy to work.

This description of discipline by Glasser may give the impression that parents should not allow freedom. However, Glasser asserts that necessary freedom for individual growth is granted to people by allowing them to make decisions and to then receive the consequences of their behavior. If, on the other hand, an individual is mentally impaired and unaware that he or she will receive either a natural reward or punishment for actions taken, that person should not be given the freedom to make such decisions.

Idea No. 6: A warm positive relationship makes discipline work.

Glasser's approach is an active approach, but its success depends on a positive relationship between child and parent. Parents must build firm, personal, and emotional relationships with their children. This is particularly true for those who have failed to develop such a relationship in the past. Parents should be responsive to their children and yet at the same time objective and rational. They should be patient enough to listen to a child's request for sympathy, but strong enough to not condone the child's misbehavior or to place responsibility on anyone other than the child.

Idea No. 7: Accept a wide range of behavior.

Also, parents should be willing to accept a wide range of behavior, even sharing and recognizing their own shortcomings. Being uncritical and understanding is essential.

This implies not becoming frightened or defensive, when confused about how to deal with a child, but having a genuine emotional involvement with the child receiving guidance. This type of relationship is oriented toward helping the child recognize and become aware of his or her own potential and strength. Consider the following example:

Shaune was teasing her sisters and being hard to live with as they were trying to get ready for school.

"Shaune, come and sit on the couch with me for a minute." She ran over and sat down.

"What's happening?" "You know, Mom." "You tell me."

"I was just teasing."

"Does that make our home happy?" "No."

"What can we do about it?" "I can stop."

"Will you?" "Yes." "Promise?" "Yes."

As she left for school after an amazing turnabout in actions, she hugged her mother and said, "I love you, Mom" and ran off happily to school.

Glasser's reality therapy technique is a process of helping children to accept responsibility for their own behavior, which will, in turn, help them to fulfill their own needs. The child is confronted with his or her behavior and helped to see the consequences of actions taken. Assisted in choosing alternative behaviors, the child is then asked to make a commitment. This approach relies on a positive, warm relationship between parent and child.

Now move to Learning Experiences 45.1, 45.2.

LEARNING EXPERIENCE 45.1

The Steps in Reality Therapy

Because the child must cooperate for this therapy to be effective, it is important that you have established a basically good relationship with your child. Once a good relationship has been established it is possible to confront the child with his or her misbehavior.

For this Learning Experience you will draw lines to connect the steps in the reality therapy to the corresponding action by the child.

Step one: The child identifies his behavior	The child makes a value judgment *not* the parent
Step Two: The child makes a value judgment of his behavior	The child formulates a plan. This plan should aim at eliminating the inappropriate behavior and make amends where necessary. It is helpful if the plan contains specifics: what, where, and when. The parent can offer help in a supportive manner. Should the child fail to implement
Step Three: The child identifies the consequences of his behavior makes a value judgment of them	The plan, both parent and child are committed to reformulate the plan together and try again.
Step Four: The Child formulates a plan and makes a commitment to follow it.	The child must identify the consequences of his actions. If the parents points out the consequences he will not be sure that the really result.
	The child identifies his own inappropriate behavior. The child, not the parent, must state what the child is doing wrong.

LEARNING EXPERIENCE 45.2

A List of Do's and Don'ts for Using Glasser's System

Mark under each list about how many times you do this in a day when parenting or interacting with children or adolescents.

Category	Do	Don't
Be personal		
Focus on Behavior		
Work in Present		
Make Value Judgment		
Make Plan to Do Better		
Avoid Excuses		

Principle 46

Parents can control television.

Idea No. 1: Television has a very strong impact on children.

Almost all homes have a television. Some researchers have pointed out that a child born today will, by the age of 18, have spent more of his life watching television than in any other activity except sleep. During the last 25 years there have been literally hundreds of studies focusing upon the particular effects of television on children. Many parents resent television because they have so little control over the content. Instead of waiting and hoping for change, there are some definite steps that can be taken to make television a positive, not a negative influence. Before considering these steps, however, a summary of parental objections to television is in order.

Idea No. 2: Parents have good reasons for being concerned about the effect of TV on their children.

Here are some parental concerns about television's impact on children:

1. Parents fear that television captures too much of their children's time. They would prefer to see their children physically active, reading, and developing talents and skills instead of hunched before a TV set.

2. Another parental concern, supported by research, is that television directly influences and teaches undesirable actions, especially aggression.

3. Parents also object to the amount and type of advertising directed toward children. Unnecessary desires and appetites are intentionally created in young children. Toys, candies, and sugar foods do not guarantee happiness as children are pressured to believe. In turn, pressure is then put on parents by children to buy unnecessary toys and games. Twenty-five percent of the industry's profit comes from programming directed at children.

4. Parents are not satisfied with the role models presented on TV. In too many shows the villain is successful for fifty minutes, only to be exposed and apprehended in the last scenes. With the airing of

more realistic movies, the examples set by heroes or heroines are especially disconcerting. An unshaven, whiskey-drinking, crude, and calloused hero in a movie is vindicated when he brutally kills evil men. The value of this social model for children is questionable and difficult for them to forget.

5. Some parents are also concerned because experience with televised violence can desensitize children to the suffering of others. Research has shown that children exposed to violent TV will react with less emotion than children who have been exposed to less violent TV programming. There is a concern that the content of our TV programs may develop a generation of children who are less sensitive to the suffering of others.

6. Many parents resent the casual and light treatment of sexual promiscuity which may be interpreted by children as acceptable. Although parents recognize that in a pluralistic society, we necessarily must confront opposing points of view, parents become justifiably upset when the prevailing values are different from their own. Most adults know their own values and are able to recognize many contrary points of view presented on TV, but children and adolescents are more vulnerable to value erosion because of what they see on TV.

7. Parents are also concerned that the type and level of moral reasoning is overly simplistic. The plots are very repetitive with evil pitted against good; for a time, evil has the upper hand, but then good conquers evil by using power and violence. Rather than solving differences through reason, the bad men are destroyed by pushing them off cliffs, or exploding their cars. Here the solution for resolving human conflict is powerfully and violently destroying the opposition.

Idea No. 3: There are many things parents can do to control television's influence on our children.

What can parents do alone? How can they counteract excessive violence, unjustified advertisement, anti-social actions, negative models, conflicting values, and low-level moral reasoning? These objectionable elements will not disappear despite commendable efforts of parent groups to get rid of them. The following are five steps that can help parents:

Step 1: Recognize what it is you don't like.

Perhaps one of the preceding criticisms is of particular concern to you. If so, then focus on its objectionable influence. It will help direct your attention and identify specific programs that are partially undesirable to you. When these have been identified, begin with Step 2.

Step 2: Guide and help children in program selection.

It would be best if young children understood that television is an invited guest into the family and that parents control and determine program selection. It is not difficult for children to understand that parents control the use of automobiles, washing machines, and most appliances. If parents will obtain a programming guide at the beginning of the week and sit down with the children to work out a viewing program, then children will believe this is the normal way to manage television. It is ideal to establish this approach when the child is young, but it can be initiated with older children if there is open discussion about program selection. It will not appear authoritarian or dictatorial if children are allowed to participate in the selection of programs.

Incidentally, there is evidence that some programs are definitely beneficial. Drs. William Meyer and Jerome Dusek 72 of Syracuse University write in their child psychology textbook, "Children who observed pro-social programs also showed an increased ability to persist at tasks, were better able to delay gratification, and obeyed rules and followed commands better." They were referring to research on programs such as "Mister Rogers.

These programs are actually designed to increase cooperation, sharing, helping, persistence, understanding feelings, delaying gratification, and valuing individuality. Other types of programs that should be scheduled are documentaries and nature programs. Recently, one parent insisted on viewing an educational telecast of a science series. He found his children, who at first were not interested, became involved as they watched the program. They began asking questions about our universe. Without his enthusiasm and advance planning, the children would never have watched this program.

Step 3: Provide discussion and counter-opinion.

In addition to program selection, a parent can watch TV with the child and then discuss highlights of the programs. The value of discussion and counter-opinion becomes important when viewing programs known to have negative content. Commercial breaks give an ideal time to discuss what is going on in the program. If the material is too volatile and controversial, it may be better to wait a day or two. At the appropriate time refer back to the program you watched together.

Even commercials can be discussed. Children take special delight in noticing adult deception and hypocrisy. As early as the first grade children are able to laugh, joke, and satire perfumes, shampoos, and make-ups that are said to transform the homely into the beautiful. A healthy skepticism can be cultivated early and children develop this criticism by endlessly role-playing the commercials.

Step 4: Provide alternative activities.

Adults as well as children will catch themselves turning on the TV when they have nothing to do. How many times have you watched a mediocre program out of habit? Too often we say, "If nothing is worth watching, then I'll do something else." Reverse the process by saying, "If there isn't something worth doing, then I'll watch TV."

By providing games, family outings, athletic events, reading hours, or even a night of cooking in the kitchen, parents can reduce the need for TV watching. Scheduling a study hour with the children early in the evening results in a positive experience for all. When a family sits down to study together, the atmosphere in the home changes; the children enjoy helping one another and sharing time together. While most parents do not have studying obligations in the evening, almost everyone enjoys magazines, books, and newspapers which can be read while children work on school assignments. By scheduling this activity during hours when there are undesirable programs, a double benefit is achieved.

Step 5: Share television experiences.

In today's world, parents and children spend less and less time together. Children go to school, women work and attend to home responsibilities, and men have their jobs. There is little time for sharing.

Television can provide these much-needed common experiences upon which to base conversation, discussion, and opinion. However, for this to work, both parents and children will often need to compromise their own preferences and watch TV together. Parents and children must sit down together so that common experiences can be shared. Sometimes adults will need to watch children's programs and sometimes children will need to watch adult programs. There is merit in having only one TV set in the home. The advantages of compromising and sharing within the family will far outweigh the pleasures of viewing only according to one's preferences. By watching common programs, conversations will be sparked. Questions can be asked about what the child or the adult would do in the same situation. These conversations will develop communication skills and thinking ability as well as clarify beliefs and values. Children can be asked to discuss their own lives in light of what they have watched on television or the news of the day. They can be asked to predict what is going to happen at the end of the show or what would happen if the family were to purchase that product. Some of the content may prove to be so controversial or interesting that the family may want to read more about it and get additional information.

It may be well to apply the old phrase, "If you can't beat them, then join them." You cannot immediately change television programming that is available for your children. So instead of developing a hopeless or resentful attitude, use the preceding steps to help develop a positive approach to television. Television can become a beneficial influence. Television can be used to bring parents and children closer together, and also to help children become informed about today's world.

Proceed now to Learning Experience 46.1.

LEARNING EXPERIENCE 46.1

Controlling Television's Influence on Our Children

Complete the following to help you plan how you will control TV's influence. Try to be more specific than the general discussion presented in the reading.

Steps to Help Parents	What Will I Do to Control TV's Influence?
Step 1 Recognize what it is you don't like.	
Step 2 Guide and help children in program selection.	
Step 3 Provide discussion and counter-opinion.	
Step 4 Provide alternative activities. Step 5	
Share television experiences.	

Principle 47

Stop fighting early.

Idea No. 1: Fighting in families is neither "normal" nor inevitable.

While many people excuse fighting as "normal," we feel that in excess it is directly connected with other problems and should not be allowed to escalate in the family.

Idea No. 2: Most parents want children to cooperate—not fight!

If the question, "What is your major problem with children?" were asked of parents, they would probably answer, "Fighting!" On the other hand, if they were asked, "What is one of the most important goals for your children?" they would probably reply "Cooperation." Cooperation involves sharing, kindness, empathy, respect, understanding rules, and delaying gratification. A child who is able to cooperate (which is more than simply obeying) is really a joy to have in a classroom or family. Children refusing to cooperate makes the job of parent or teacher much more difficult. In addition, to be successful in adult life, children must learn to cooperate. Fighting should not be expected or considered desirable or inevitable.

Idea No. 3: There are many different unnecessary reasons why children fight.

Why do children (and older people) fight? We see young children "jostling" and having a great time doing so. This is more of a physical exercise and usually does not involve feelings of hostility or anger. There are other types of fighting, however, that are physically and emotionally damaging to the child as well as extremely irritating to adults. Ask most teachers, and they will tell you that the incessant in- class fighting between two or more children is almost intolerable. To help parents understand this intolerable situation, we have listed possible explanations for why children fight.

Fighting is a form of communication. Especially for young children, fighting is one of the ways in which they communicate. Because they have not learned other more efficient and desirable forms of communication, the young toddler will fight to get what he wants and to influence others.

Fighting is expected. Sometimes children are expected to fight. Boys, at a very young age in particular, may be taught by their dads to "fight it out" and not let the other guy "get away with that."

Fighting draws attention. Children fight to gain the attention of parent or teacher. Although reactions on the part of the adult are usually irritation or annoyance, as in the following illustration; they are nevertheless attention-seeking.

Mother was talking on the telephone. Jani and Heather were playing with the paper dolls. "That's mine!" shouted Heather, taking away one of the paper dolls. "No it isn't, it's mine!" shouted Jani. The girls fought and fought over the paper doll until it was torn. Jani started to cry, and Heather started yelling, "It's all your fault! You tore the paper doll, and it was mine!"

Mother put the phone down on her shoulder and shouted, "Girls, stop fighting. Can't you see I'm talking on the telephone?" The girls continued to argue over who had torn the doll and whose it was until finally Mother got off the phone and gave them both spankings.

It appears from this illustration that not only were the girls frustrated about the paper doll and about tearing it, but they were also trying to draw their mother's attention. Mother, of course, gave them that desired attention which reinforced their attention-getting behavior of fighting while she is on the telephone.

Children fight because of frustration. Frequently, because they do not know any other way to take out their frustration, children act aggressively and fight with other children. The source of the frustration can be caused by: 1) a deficient satisfaction of physical needs (not enough sleep, food, warmth); 2) lack of the ability to complete a task successfully; or 3) inadequate satisfaction of emotional, creative, or intellectual needs.

Children fight because of modeling. A tremendous amount of research has been conducted on modeling aggressive behavior. Children do act more aggressively after watching an aggressive model. The theory is that children will fight more when seeing their parents fight and argue.

Children also would tend to fight more after viewing television in which aggression is displayed in cartoon form and real-life dramas.

Children fight because of permissiveness. Parents and teachers who allow fighting to occur, indirectly encourage more fighting. This idea appears to be in contrast with the theory that children fight for attention, and if paid that attention, fighting will continue. However, we are not advocating that the child be given direct, or individual attention, which is what he or she may want. The important thing to remember is not to take sides in the fight. It is almost impossible to know all the details of a fight; therefore, adults should treat children as a group in trying to resolve a fight. For example, a teacher might say to two boys who are fighting over a truck, "I can see that you boys are not willing to work things out with the truck. I'll have to put it up on the shelf. Maybe you can try again tomorrow." The teacher did not try to figure out which boy had the truck first, and therefore did not take sides.

Another statement the adult could make is "I'm sorry you two are having trouble over the paper dolls, but I'm sure you can work it out between you."

When the fighting gets too rough and either teacher or parents feel it should be stopped, they should again treat the children as a group. "You will both need to come in now since you can't play together in the sandbox," "You boys can choose to stop fighting or go to bed," or "You'll have to stop fighting now. You can each go to your rooms to calm down a bit."

Children usually are happy that teachers or parents set some limits and do not allow the fighting to continue—especially the child who is getting hurt.

Idea No. 4: Children can learn alternate responses rather than fighting.

There are alternatives parents can use to help children resolve conflict with fighting:

Emotional Aggression. When children are frustrated, they need to draw from responses other than physical aggression to cope with their frustration. One alternative to physical aggression is emotional aggression which, hopefully, will turn out to be a healthy confrontation. Children need to express their frustrations in a healthy way by using verbalization with strong emotion, if necessary. Here's an example:

Angela finger-painted a pretty picture at the table where she was working. Rusty, who was sitting next to Angela, messed up her picture. Angela became so angry she began beating her hands on the table and splashing finger paint all over Rusty's face.

"What's going on?" asked the teacher.

"Rusty messed up my picture," cried Angela, "and now it is all ruined."

The teacher wanted to help the children see that fighting was not the way to solve the problem. "Angela, can you think of a better way to let Rusty know you didn't like what he did to your picture?"

"No," said Angela. "I just don't like him any more. He ruined my picture."

The teacher persisted. "Angela, can you think of a way to tell Rusty you didn't like what he did without splashing paint all over him?"

"I guess so," said Angela. "I don't like what you did to my picture, Rusty. I worked really hard on it and now it's all ruined. Would you like somebody to do that to your picture?"

"No," said Rusty ashamedly. "I'm sorry, Angela. I didn't mean to make you sad. I just wanted some of your finger paint."

"Will you promise not to do it again?" asked Angela forgivingly. "Yes, I promise. I won't mess your picture up again," said Rusty.

"There now," said the teacher. "Wasn't that a better way than fighting?"

Idea No. 5: Cooperation is a very desirable alternative to fighting.

Encourage Cooperation. Another alternate response to be encouraged is cooperation. Children should be encouraged to see that because of cooperation, two can be happy rather than one happy and one sad. When children cooperate, no one loses and everyone gains. As an example, two children are building with Legos, but neither child has enough Legos to build a big tower. If, however, they work together and build the tower as a team, they not only have enough Legos to build the tower, but they have a good time building it. The experience becomes not only physically and intellectually stimulating and creative, but socializing as well.

Help children understand that life is not always fair. Even though we would like it to be, life is not always fair, and we can't guarantee a just and fair environment. It is impossible, for example, for parents to treat their children equally at all times, just as it is impossible for teachers to treat children in the classroom equally at all times. Sometimes children do something wrong and do not get punished. Other children see the situation as unfair and attempt to "take things into their own hands." It should be explained to children that this is not their responsibility. Consider, for example, a child who broke the convertible top on the family car by turning on the switch when the top was fastened. "I'm going to beat him up," said his brother. "Now we can't put the top down until we get it fixed." Mother quietly reminds the protesting boy that she will take care of it, not him, and that "Life's not fair."

Now proceed to Learning Experience 47.1.

LEARNING EXPERIENCE 47.1

Steps for Teaching Children Not to Fight

Below are some ideas or suggestions for teaching children to **not fight.** For each of them give a story of how you have seen this done or how you think it might be done. Include in your narrative a statement indicating how this suggestion or step can lead to less fighting.

Idea 1:   Recognize that fighting in families is not normal and communicate this to your children.

Idea 2:   Teach children cooperation.

Idea 3:   Teach children better ways to communicate.

Idea 4:   Don't let children fight it out.

Idea 5:   Teach children positive ways to get attention.

Idea 6:   Teach children better ways to handle frustration.

Idea 7:   Do not model parental aggressiveness for your children.

Idea 8:   Do not allow fighting to continue.

Idea 9:   Do not take sides in a fight.

Idea 10:   Teach children alternate responses to physical aggression.

Idea 11:   Help children find constructive outlets for aggressive behavior.

Idea 12:   Help children accept that life is not always fair.

SUMMARY

Instructions: Mark *a* if the statement is true and *b* if it is false. Submit to Instructor.

1. Continuous fighting in families is neither normal nor inevitable.

2. Fighting sometimes occurs because it is expected or to get attention.

3. Fighting is never a form of communication and does not occur in more permissive homes.

4. If children understand that life is fair, they will be less likely to be aggressive.

5. Fighting can be reduced by teaching cooperation.

6. In Reality Therapy there are four basic steps: a) the child must make a value judgment about misbehavior; b) the child must identify the future results of behavior; c) the child must make better plans for future behavior; and 4) the child must make a commitment.

7. When using Reality Therapy the relationship is not important and one should not accept a wide range of behaviors.

8. Parents' reasons for being concerned about the negative influence of television include: a) time; b) teaches undesirable actions; c) the types of advertisements; and d) the kind of role models. This listing is complete.

9. Suggestions given in the text to help parents control television are: a) recognize what it is that the parents don't like; b) guide program selection; c) provide discussion and counter-opinion; d) provide alternative activities; and e) share the television experiences.

10. Although parents are concerned about television, there is not much evidence that television has a significant effect on children's behavior.

LESSON TWELVE

Establishing Morality and Values

After you have successfully completed this lesson, you should be able to do the following:

Identify and use five steps for developing an internal morality.

Demonstrate the importance of teaching values.

Show how you can develop positive values naturally by creating a happy family.

Realize the widespread use of prayer in the United States and the value of prayer for parenting.

Principle 48

Developing a morality based on feelings for others

In our family we have the usual problems like every other family but we always know we love one another, whenever one child has a bad day or is treated unfairly you can be sure that his brothers and sisters will try to help and comfort. This pattern starts at an age when children first learn to talk and increases into adulthood.

Compare this family with the frequently heard words below:

"But he was such a good child, I don't understand how he could have turned out so bad." This child may have been highly rewarded for his good behavior and punished for bad, rather than being allowed to learn by having freedom to make mistakes during childhood. He did not acquire controls from within because he was being controlled from without. When this outward control is removed, an internal personal guidance system that could have come from low-power disciplinary techniques is lacking. Such techniques provide opportunities for acquiring inner controls based on logic or rationality, awareness of feelings, and concern for others. Note not only the absence of coercion but also the necessity for providing a growth-promoting environment with standards, expectations, and values.

Idea No. 1: Help children gain inner controls for moral behavior. Often, obtaining desired moral behavior is somewhere "up in the clouds." We hope that through the techniques and problem-solving tasks presented, ways of achieving desired moral behavior can be brought "down to earth." The following account shows how to do this.

In my family, Mother was generally the one who was home and to whom we went to receive permission to do things with our friends or to go to special activities. Often, however, she would have us wait until our father got home and then ask him (if it was something really important). What Dad said was the final word, and we all just accepted it.

One Sunday afternoon when I was about seven years old, one of my good friends called and asked me if I would go to a movie with her that afternoon. I was really excited because movies with friends were rare since I usually only went with my sister. I really wanted to go, but our religious family did not believe in movies on Sunday. I went into the kitchen where Mom and Dad were to see if they would let me go.

Ordinarily, my parents would have made a decision and then either said I could or couldn't go. Dad changed his format this time. I guess he decided I was old enough to begin taking responsibility for myself. He told me it was my decision—I could go to the movie today, or I could stay home and do something else. Ordinarily, I would have been thrilled to have such trust placed in me, but I wasn't; I didn't want the responsibility. I knew it was Sunday, and I had been taught that movies weren't appropriate for the Sabbath. I didn't want to decide between what was right and what I wanted, but Dad was firm. I would have to decide. I knew if I said "no," I would have to explain to my friend, and I couldn't blame my parents. But if I had said "yes," I would feel guilty because again, it was my decision. I deliberated quite awhile and finally decided not to go. I was by no means happy with my decision, and really resented my parents

Idea No. 2: Help and allow children to make the hard decisions.

Part of a child's ability to develop a morality based on feelings for others involves helping the child understand others. How do children learn to understand others? Why do some people never learn to understand others? "He just doesn't understand me," and "She has no feelings for others," exemplify the way many of us have felt in some situations. Typically, little children lack an understanding of others.[88] They are egocentric, not having had enough experience in the world to relate to the needs and problems of other people. It is our firm belief, however, that young children can be helped to understand other's feelings.

Idea No. 3: There are five steps for developing internal morality.

The following techniques are proposed:

1. Calling attention to the needs of another individual. "Homer was very *hungry* and you ate all the sausages before he could get one."

2. Calling attention to the *feelings* of another individual. "Homer felt very sad when you ate all the sausages. He was hungry and now he doesn't have anything to eat."

3. Help the child try to *put himself in the shoes of the other individual.*

   "Try to think what it would be like if you were very hungry and you wanted a sausage very much and someone ate them all. Would you be happy or sad? Would you still be hungry?"

4. Help the child *discover* his feelings but avoid lecturing or telling the child how he would feel if the same thing happened to him. Ask the child questions which are neither probing, sarcastic, nor humiliating. The tone of voice is important in helping the child discover feelings on his own. "I wonder how it would feel to be hungry and plan on eating sausages and then find out that someone already ate them all? I wonder if you would feel happy or sad? I wonder if you would still be hungry? Would you feel angry?"

   Don't Say:

   "I'm sure if someone ate all your sausages that you Would feel sad or angry. It's not nice to eat other people's food when they are planning on eating it. You would be very angry if someone did that to you."

The "Don't Say" example tells the child how you think he should feel and does not allow the child the opportunity to discover these feelings on *his own*.

5. Lastly, help children act upon their feelings of empathy. In other words, helping a child learn that empathetic feelings are important is not enough, a person must *respond* to those feelings. *Altruism* is the term used to describe behaviors that relieve the distress of another individual. This altruism is behavior motivated by the child's feelings of empathy and an honest desire to help relieve another's distress, not by a desire for social approval, expected rewards, or fear of punishment. The expression of altruism is a mature moral response, not typically developed at a young age. Movement towards altruism can be made, however, by first, helping the child develop a feeling of empathy and, second by encouraging the child to *act* upon that feeling. If a child sees another child fall off a tricycle and feels empathy for the hurt child, he should then be encouraged to respond by going to the hurt child and attending or get help attending to any injuries. A young child can and often does show altruistic responses. Adults need to be attentive to these responses by rewarding the child and helping him to feel good for responding to the needs of another in distress. The development of empathy and feeling for another individual is incomplete without acting upon that feeling. In the illustration used above with Homer and the sausages, an adult's response might be:

"I wonder if we could think of a way to help Homer so he won't feel sad or hungry any more. Can we find him some more sausages, or can you think of something else we could do?"

By providing the preceding experiences, many young children will be able to feel empathy and to express altruistic responses even though both are considered to be mature responses:

In Learning Experience 48.1, you can practice using these steps.

LEARNING EXPERIENCE 48.1

Developing Internal Morality Based on Feelings for Others

In this Learning Experience use the five steps to teach a moral response for each of the following situations.

A selfish child or adolescent

1.

2.

3.

4.

5.

A child or adolescent who teases

1.

2.

3.

4.

5.

A child who steals from other children

1.

2.

3.

4.

5.

A bully or aggressive teenager

1.

2.

3.

4.

5.

Principle 49

It is crucial to teach values.

My parents never really taught me any values because I guess they thought they didn't need to. I guess they figured that our church would tell me all I needed to know and what they didn't teach, I could see from their actions. They also believe that I have the right to make my own values and beliefs, but if I go against them I have found that they criticize me and will not support me.

Idea No. 1: Most parents believe that teaching values is important but many do not.

Some parents are reluctant to teach values to their children. The story above points out two possible reasons: 1) some parents don't think there is a need for them to teach values; and 2) some parents don't believe they have the right to teach values. Because of the public alarm about declining moral values in our society and the lack of moral instruction in the schools, most parents today would probably say something else. So ingrained in some people is the idea that no one should impose their values on someone else that many parents have lost the vision of their opportunity and responsibility to teach values to their children.

Idea No. 2: Our modern life makes teaching values more needed and more difficult.

Additionally, when parents do try to teach values, they run into difficulty with their youth because of widespread changes in moral values as portrayed in media and society at large. Some adolescents become so argumentative that parents wish they hadn't even tried. Because of a disagreement about moral values the parents may find their child not only criticizing their moral viewpoint but also rejecting the parents as well.

Teaching moral values is more difficult today. In the past there was more agreement on a common set of moral values that people generally accepted. Society is now more diversified than in the past and also more polarized in terms of values. No longer can the home count on the school or other community institutions to teach moral values to their children. At a time when parents spend less time at home with their children there is an even greater need for parents to provide a moral foundation.

One of the difficulties today is that not only are there multiple beliefs to choose from, but many parents are not quite sure what they believe. If the parent has only a weak affiliation and a moderate commitment to religious beliefs, a religious message to be taught to the children lacks a strong direction and meaning. The case below illustrates the situation where parents do have definite beliefs which provide stability for teaching of moral values to children:

My parents have always had their own beliefs and values and seemed quite sure that they were correct. Therefore, they had very little trouble communicating them to us and hoping that we would adopt them as our own. They did this in two ways. First, they would be open and would just state what their expectations of us were. Second, they would encourage behavior in us that would indicate that the beliefs were present in us.

Idea No. 3: Effective teaching of values and beliefs is done by explaining and modeling the desired behaviors.

Two basic steps for parents to remember when trying to influence the development of a value system in teens are as follows:

1. First, the parent must directly state his beliefs; and,

2. The parent must "practice what he preaches" or be a model for the behavior he wishes his children to adopt. Setting an example almost always has to be congruent with advocating a belief.

My parents used both models and explanations. I always knew what my parents expected of me because of their examples and yet they didn't force their beliefs and values on me. They would talk to me and explain how they felt, and I could tell what I should be doing from the way that they behaved and the things they did. I just always seemed to know what they believed, and this influenced me

Idea No. 4: Values and beliefs are best taught informally on a day- to-day basis.

Teaching of values and beliefs is best done informally as the family interacts on a day-to-day basis. One woman reported as follows:

My parents communicated to me—to all of us—the values and beliefs that they had through their example and by telling us. I remember many evenings where we would discuss beliefs that we all held. Our entire family will often have discussions of how we feel about certain things and about what our expectations are regarding different matters. Thus, we know firsthand the beliefs that our parents have and how they expect us to act, plus we are able to share with them how we feel about things. There have been times when we have disagreed and yet through these discussions we were able to come to terms with our disagreements and work them out before they worked into explosive actions.

Idea No. 5: Extended family members can sometimes assist in teaching values.

Parents often need help in teaching moral values to their children. Sometimes the help can come from a member of the extended family or a trusted neighbor. Especially when the adults and children are not in agreement about moral values, others outside the immediate family may be very helpful in communicating to the child that there are others besides his/her parents who feel that way.

The following story shows how the value of cleanliness was taught to a young woman by her mother through being introduced to her grandmother's beliefs.

My mother was very concerned with cleanliness. When was in my teens, my mother had a rough time teaching me this on her own. She knew that I really respect my great-grandmother, so when she emphasized to me the importance of changing my sheets once a week she would always remind me of how important it was to my grandmother. This got my attention and gave me a greater desire to keep my room in the condition that my great-grandmother would be proud of.

Idea No. 6: Children want to meet parental expectations.

A positive approach is beneficial in teaching expectations. Simply changing the language helps. Instead of shouting "stop all the noise" ask children to "speak quietly." Instead of saying "Don't come home late," ask children to "Be home on time." And, instead of saying, "Don't be mean to your brother," say "Treat your brother the way you would like to be treated." If something negative must be said, refrain from repeating it over and over again. The following story gives an example of the positive approach:

My parents paid special attention to things I did after only being told once or not at all. As a result, I remember feeling positive about filling their expectations, and even listening very carefully to notice the things they would want me to do. This didn't always work, but I remember the feeling of wanting to fill their expectations. Part of the reward I got was to feel responsible.

Idea No. 7: Touching stories that children can relate to are more effective than preaching.

Another effective technique is to appeal to feelings rather than to logic. A saying is, "A man convinced against his will is of the same opinion still." Trying to produce real change by logical argument is often quite futile. Using touching stories that children can relate to is often more effective. A mother used this approach in the story below:

My children were driving and learning to drive when there was a great deal of public concern over the results of driving and drinking. Two locally popular teens had been senselessly killed—victims of an intoxicated driver. Newspapers printed emotional stories of their lives and the success they might have achieved, and my teenagers could relate to the story.

One evening we sat around the table and I read to them the accounts of the story. By the time we were through, the kids felt like they knew the teenagers that had lost their lives. The article talked about the agony of the other driver. There was no preaching done by me or my husband. The children "ate it up." There were tears from my daughter and red eyes from my son.

Without preaching and by taking advantage of a current tragedy, my children developed strong feelings about the effects of alcohol and the senselessness of driving under its influence.

Idea No. 8: Goals and expectations are best set together with parents and child.

Setting standards and expectations should be done jointly with parents and children. In the following story a young man shares his father's handling of a problem in a way that is fondly appreciated by the son:

The time I can think of that my parents set a standard for me was when I was in junior high. I brought home a report card that had a "D" on it. When my father looked over my card, he called me in and talked to me about my grades. He pointed out that he was pleased with my good grades, but he told me that a "D" wasn't an acceptable grade. He said that he knew that I could do better than that.

This showed me two things. It showed me that Dad was interested and concerned about all of my grades, and it showed that he thought I had the ability to attain grades of a higher level. After we talked about the classes I was taking and what I should be doing in those classes. Then we set a level that was acceptable to both of us.

LEARNING EXPERIENCE 49.1

Teaching Values to Children

After reading the following statements, answer true or false by circling the corresponding letter.

1. T F Most parents don't realize or believe that they must teach values.

2. T F Our modern society provides many ways to help parents teach values.

3. T F It is better that a parent refrain from directly telling his beliefs to a child.

4. T F Explaining values is more important than example.

5. T F Values and beliefs should not be taught informally.

6. T F It is better that parents do the teaching of values and leave other relatives out in order to avoid contradictions.

7. T F Children usually dislike meeting parental expectations.

8. T F If preaching doesn't work, try stories which are the second best method for teaching values.

9. T F Parents should decide on the standards and not be influenced by their children.

LEARNING EXPERIENCE 49.2

Making Your Own Plan to Teach Values

As you can see there is no one surefire way to help your children acquire values and morals. Methods seem to vary from parent to parent. However, successful parents must be doing something right. In the space below create and outline your own theory or how you will go about instilling in your children or helping them acquire good values.

Principle 50

Morality occurs naturally in a happy family.

We lived on a farm and being the sixth of seven children, there was plenty to keep my younger brother and I busy. We played for hours in the hay or the attic of the barn. My parents were always loving, and I always wanted to please them.

At times, I suppose, I felt obligated to do what was right and make them happy, but this pressure did not stem from them but from myself. I recall being up to something all of the time. I loved to clean my brothers' rooms, to rub their backs, to vacuum (strange child?). All these things made me happy. I had everything I needed and most of what I wanted.

Generally, I was just a happy little kid. Being out in the country is the only way to go. I hope that I can raise my kids there. Freedom comes to mind as another very strong emotion (is it an emotion?). I could do most anything, go anywhere (down to the dump, up to the lake, to the railroad tracks where we would put pennies on the track). We climbed up the roof of the barn, had dirt-clod fights. Looking back, I'm amazed that my mom let us do the things we did—we could have gotten hurt! But it was great. . . happy . . . carefree.

Idea No. 1: Moral behavior can occur naturally.

The student above told of the happiness of a childhood in the country, while the following story tells of the benefits of life in a large family. In this story and the one below good behavior occurred very naturally. Why?

My family is a large and close one with five girls and three boys. Many times we would go to a movie or out to eat with a group of three or four of the older children, each of us bringing a friend. We got along well and felt comfortable in each other's company. Since we were so close, our friends became close to other members of my family, and I became close to some of my brothers' and sisters' friends. This, in a way, was our group, and we all felt we belonged to this group. I especially sought the approval of my brothers and sisters and wanted to be considered one of the Tuckett children. My older brothers set good examples for me and expected me to set a good example for my younger brother and sisters. All in all, my group which was mostly my siblings and their friends, was very important to me.

Another story tells of the importance of fun:

One of the most powerful emotions in my childhood was humor, or happiness. My family has always been really fun with a lot of bantering and joking going on. Dad used to play with us, chasing us around the house as we screamed and laughed. He used to chase us and stick our stocking-feet into the sink under the running water or pour red ink into our bath water. We were almost always happy and laughing. My mother always played along with Dad's pranks, and sometimes even got an ice cube down her back!

I don't quite know what emotion constitutes all our playfulness, but I know that without it home life would have been very drab. My brother continues on the tradition but the roles have switched. My brother chases my mother around the house with a glass of water to retaliate for her spraying him with the ironing bottle. All in all, my home is one that I still love to go back to because of the happy, loving atmosphere.

Idea No. 2: A high ratio of positive to negative emotions is the key.

Perhaps the most important indicator of a healthy emotional life is that ratio of positive emotions to negative or disintegrative emotions. For example, the child's life should be one that primarily contains love, affection, sympathy, joy, contentment, and security as opposed to hate, hostility, despair, remorse, and fear.

In spite of our efforts to parent our children in the best way we can, we should not become so consumed with finding some elusive "how to parent" technique that we forget that family relationships are the essential element to develop moral behavior. Children who grow up in a happy home environment will not only share the happiness with their parents but share their values also. Morality, therefore, is more likely to occur naturally in a happy home atmosphere.

Idea No. 3: Happy homes are more likely to produce moral children.

Four steps proposed for bringing about strong character and moral behavior in a natural way are described below.

1. Develop love and a sense of belonging in the home.

2. State expectations and beliefs clearly.

3. Follow-through with checking up, rewards, natural consequences, and standing firm.

4. Be positive and provide a happy home.

As indicated in the steps above, two of the important ingredients are love and belonging and a happy home. Parents who guide their children through love, respect, and a sense of belonging are able to influence their children's behavior in substantial ways. On the other hand, parents who try to gain compliance only through force often find that youth learn how to comply on a surface level to avoid punishment but do not really develop moral characters as intended by their parents.

Idea No. 4: Don't underestimate the power of love, expectations, follow-through, and the sense of belonging.

Many parents underestimate the power of their family group to meet the belonging needs of their children. This is a first step in developing a strong conscience, character, and positive morality. The good feelings engendered by this sense of belonging is the first step in the natural process of moral development.

Idea No. 5: Humor is important.

Humor and other positive emotions are important for children to encounter. However, it is important for parents to let their children experience the normal ups and downs of emotional and social life without excessively shielding them from negative experiences.

Idea No. 6: The positive climate is still the key to successful and moral children.

Emotional Stability: In general, a positive emotional climate in the home is the single most important influencing factor for stable emotional responding. Particularly important is the experience of being accepted by others, producing an emotional feeling that "I belong," "I'm worthwhile," or "I'm loved and a part of this group." Sometimes an extra effort is required on the part of parents to bolster self-esteem when children feel inadequate.

When I was growing up I was always taught to have a positive self-image. This created in me the knowledge that if I wanted to do something and tried hard enough I would be able to accomplish it. My parents always tried to put trust and confidence in me to assure me that I was capable of performing well. In the fourth grade my teacher was going to hold me back because of poor reading skills. She approached my parents about this possibility and told my parents that unless I showed vast improvement, I would have to repeat fourth grade. My parents came to me and expressed confidence in me and told me that if I worked hard I would not have to stay back. The possibility of failing placed an extreme strain on my self-esteem. But, through my parents' reassurance, I was able to improve my skills, and by the end of the fourth grade I was at the top of my class in reading and I felt really good about myself.

This child needed his parents to help him maintain a positive self-image. In the process the child acquired virtues and character. Sometimes the direct path is not the best. So it is with morality. By providing a solid family experience full of positive feelings and joy, values, and morality mutually unfold.

Proceed now to Learning Experience 50.1.

LEARNING EXPERIENCE 50.1

Choose the answer that best fits your feelings about each of the statements below:

Key   **1 = Never agree**   **2 = Sometimes agree**

        3 = Usually agree   **4 = Always agree**

1. There exist many different examples of how moral behavior can occur naturally.

     1   2   3   4

2. A good way to find out the level of someone's emotional health is to compare the ratio of positive emotions to negative or disintegrative emotions.

     1   2   3   4

3. Naturally-occurring morality is most likely to occur in a home where there is a "happy" home atmosphere.

     1   2   3   4

4. Developing love and a sense of belonging in the home is a way of building moral development.

     1   2   3   4

5. When encouraging morality with children, parents should state expectations clearly and follow-through with rewarding, checking up, natural consequences, and standing firm.

     1   2   3   4

6. A major contributing factor to a strong conscience, character, and positive morality is the power of belonging.

     1   2   3   4

7. Fun and humor in the home are important ingredients in the family's happiness.

     1   2   3   4

8. Children should be given the right and opportunity to feel any emotion.

     1   2   3   4

9. Parents can help children handle negative emotional experiences by discussing their emotions with them.

    1   2   3   4

10. A positive emotional climate in the home has to be the most important influencing factor for stable emotional responding.

    1   2   3   4

Principle 51

The world's most used parenting techniques

When I was fourteen, my best friend and her family invited me to go on their family vacation with them for the whole summer. I was really excited about the idea, and so I asked my mom if I could go. She said that she didn't think it was a good idea. So I appealed to my dad and he and my mom asked for a few days to talk it over before giving me a final decision. About a week later my parents told me they had booked a reservation and I could go. I guessed my dad had been able to convince my mom about all the good experiences I could have because there were by far more positives than negatives. So, to say the least, I was thrilled.

For the next month it was all my best friend and I could talk about— how great this vacation was going to be, and how much fun we were going to have. About a week before we were to leave, I started to pack. Then, three days before I left, I came home and found my parents sitting on the couch waiting for me. They told me they had canceled my flight and that they didn't want me to go. I was so devastated and angry at them—especially my mom. She explained that for the last month she had been living with such an uneasy feeling about me going on this trip that she couldn't let me go through with it. So my dad told her that if she felt that strongly about it, then maybe they should listen, so they canceled my trip.

It took about two weeks to get over my anger, but I ended up getting my first job that summer and that was really important to my growth. This was a memorable summer for me, and I'm glad now that I didn't go. And I will never know what would have happened if I had gone, but maybe it would have been a bad experience.

Idea No. 1: Parents often use intuition in guiding their children.

In a modern world of science, facts, and logical proofs, intuition is too often looked down upon. However, if you were to read college textbooks on problem-solving, scientific discovery, or learning, there is ample evidence to show that creative discoveries often result from the use of intuition. Scientists and creative people report that they were often able to discover new and unexpected solutions that fall into the category of being intuitive.

Idea No. 2: Inspiration has saved many families from disaster.

Now let's see again how to profitably use intuition in the parenting process by reading the following example:

Before I was born, my family consisted of my father, my mother, and my brother, Mark. One day, while my father was at work, my mother and Mark were home, doing the daily tasks and playing, respectively. Mark was around two years old at the time. Suddenly, my mother stopped everything, because she knew something was not right. At that moment she heard Mark's small voice saying, "Mama," yet he was nowhere in sight. Mark had quickly wandered off, and my mother had no idea where he was, but she knew he needed help.

At the back end of the property there was a fence and beyond that a swiftly flowing irrigation ditch. Without stopping to think, my mother ran for the ditch and hurdled the fence (quite an amazing feat for a skilled athlete, let alone my petite, lady-like, and reserved mother). There she found Mark who had indeed fallen into the ditch. Somehow he had gotten through the fence and was now in the ditch, barely hanging on to the some weeds on the side. Mother was able to grab him just as he lost his grip or he would have been swept away by the current.

The most awe-inspiring part of this story is that my mother could never have heard Mark from such a far distance with him in the ditch and her inside the house. Yet, she knew where Mark was, that he needed help, and she was able to get to him and save him.

Idea No. 3: Many mothers and fathers report that prayer is important in parenting.

The January 30, 1995 issue of *Time magazine*, reported that 65 percent of American adults say they have had one of their prayers answered specifically. We believe that the percentage would be even higher if they had asked only parents. Parents may pray more than anyone else. Why? Because they have more to pray about! In our research with 65 parents who had successfully raised at least one adolescent we asked, "To what extent has prayer been important in your parenting?" The results were as follows:

Importance of Prayer to Parents by Percentage

	Father	Mother
Extremely Important	38%	54%
Important	17%	32%
Not Important	41%	13%
No Response	03%	02%

The following two stories were given by students in one of our workshops:

They did not seem to be an outstanding family. She attended church irregularly, and he did not attend at all. She had a small responsibility in the local church group. But, I noticed that all of their children seemed to be turning out very well, and I wondered why-especially when so many others in our neighborhood were struggling with their children. Then she spoke at a women's meeting at church and answered my question about her success as a parent: "When I was raising adolescents I spent a lot of time on my knees," she reported.

Idea No. 4: Many parents have found that turning to God has helped their adolescent children turn around.

Ellen was a wife and mother. Her husband was an architect and so their family was pretty well off. Ellen had two children, Anne and Sean. The family wasn't what you would call religious. Ellen believed in God, but her husband was an atheist.

The children's growing up years were happy but when Anne, the oldest child, got to junior high, things started to change. Anne got involved with the wrong crowd at school. Ellen and her husband were morally upright people and they had tried to teach their children morality and values. So when Anne got involved with the kids whose values and beliefs were different from the family's, Anne's parents got worried. This situation continued and, in spite of everything Anne's parents tried to do to help Anne change her course, finally Anne left home.

Ellen did not know what to do. She began to turn to God for help. She prayed for Anne all the time and before long Anne returned home and things changed. Anne enrolled in school and got a job.

Idea No. 5: Many youth report that religious beliefs and faith in God have helped them through difficult times.

The following story shows the value of prayer from the child's perspective:

Just this semester I was going through some very serious decision making, so serious that it was not only affecting me mentally but also physically and spiritually. It came to the point where I decided to withdraw from school and go back to New Zealand to take time out, think, clear my mind, and also maintain my integrity with the school because I wasn't doing well in any of my classes.

I called home and told my mom that I'd be home or wanted to come home in two weeks. My mom, with tears in her voice, told me not to give up, but to stay at BYU-Hawaii. I didn't want to, but she asked me to pray and fast for answers and to just wait until the end of the month. If nothing changed, I was to call home again and she'd bring me home.

Well, little things started to happen that week that just seemed to answer my problems. I had prayed a lot before, but because my situation had discouraged me so much, I had stopped that week. But my mom was praying and fasting for me at home that everything would work out. I'm still here now and everything literally fell into place for me, and now life is not only back to normal, but better. I'll be getting married this summer. I guess the Lord knew how to settle all my problems and provided a way that would calm me and bring peace to my mom. He answered her prayers and helped me.

Having read the above examples of the affects of prayer, please proceed to Learning Experience 51.1.

LEARNING EXPERIENCE 51.1

How Prayer Helps in Parenting

Even if you don't believe in God or a supreme being, you may want to ask yourself these questions about prayer and parenting. You may still find prayer a very important tool in your family and your life. Intuition, meditation, or introspection are also useful and have similarities to prayer. Please answer the following questions as indicated.

1. What percentage of mothers and fathers do you think focus their prayers on their children?

2. Do you think people who ask for help in parenting have an advantage over those who do not ask? If your answer is "yes," please explain why. If your answer is "no," please explain what you think is likely to happen when a person prays for the welfare of a child.

3. Could the prayer of a sincere parent result in a positive experience even if the parent did not have a strong belief in God or a Supreme Being? Please explain.

4. Circle the letter for any of the following statements that indicate ways in which a parent's prayer might be answered.

    a. Feeling that something should or should not be done.

    b. A logical and clear plan of action comes to mind.

    c. A change of heart takes place in the child.

    d. The parent seems to have additional strength and energy to perform the parenting tasks.

    e. An unexpected form of additional help appears.

    f. Extra resources to help the parent are discovered.

    g. The parent feels comforted and reassured.

    h. All of the above and more.

5.   Circle the letter for any of the following statements which apply to parents' prayers.

   a.   There is an authoritative source.

   b.   They are inexpensive.

   c.   They address a whole range of problems.

   d.   They can be used anywhere and at anytime.

   e.   They are available to everyone.

SUMMARY

Instructions: Mark *a* if the statement is true and *b* if it is false

1. The five steps for developing an internal morality are: a) calling attention to the needs of another; b) calling attention to the feelings of another; c) putting oneself in the shoes of the other; d) helping the child discover feelings without lecturing and telling; and e) helping children act upon their feelings.

2. Many parents don't realize or believe that they must teach values.

3. Explaining values is more important than example.

4. Values and beliefs are so important that they should not be taught informally.

5. If preaching doesn't work, use stories which are almost as good a method.

6. Morality can occur naturally in a happy family even without formal instruction.

7. The ratio of positive to negative emotions is a key element in establishing a healthy morality.

8. Most parents do not like and do not use religion or prayer in raising their children.

9. Parenting prayers are usually answered in a very clear, expected way.

10. Parenting prayers were recommended as the world's best parenting technique.

SOURCES CITED

"Dear reader, I ask you to please look past some of the problems in these references as I am unable to fully address them at this time. However they still do provide theory and data upon which the content of this book rests."

1. Sears, R., Maccoby, E., and Levin, H. 1957. *Patterns of Childrearing.* Evanston, IL: Row Peterson.

2. McClelland, D. C., et al. 1977. Making it to maturity. *Psychology Today* 12:53.

3. Birch, G., Thomas, A., and Chess, S 1970. The Origins of Personality. *Scientific American*

   223:102-109.

4. Satir, V. *Peoplemaking.* 1972. Palo Alto, CA: Science and Behavior Books, 211-213.

5. Baumrind, D. 1971. Current patterns of parental authority. *Developmental Psychology Monographs* 4:101.

6. Bell, R. Q., and Harper, L. V. 1977. *Child Effects on Adults. Harper Publishing*

7. Belsky, J., Steinberg, L., and Draper, P. 1991. Childhood Experiences, interpersonal and reproductive strategy: An evaluative theory of socialization. *Child Development* 62:647-670.

8. Leifer, M. 1980. *Psychological Effects of Motherhood: A Study of First Pregnancy.* New York: Praeger.

9. Kitzinger, S. 1983. *The Complete Book of Pregnancy and Childbirth.* New York: Knopf.

10. Ainsworth, M. D. S. 1973. The development of infant-mother attachment. In Cladwell, B. M. and Riciutti, H. N. (eds.) *Review of Child Development Research. Vol. 111.* Chicago: University of Chicago Press.

11. Egeland, B., and Farber, E. A. 1984. Infant-mother attachment: Factors related to its develoment and changes over time. *Child Development* 55:753-771.

12. Egeland B. and Sroufe, L. A. 1981. Attachment and early maltratment. *Child Development* 52: 44-52.

Approximately 97 men and 133 women had complete data for these questions, so there are slight variations. The average number of children in these families was two; the ages of the eldest children ranged from three to sixty. Eighty-five percent described themselves as middle class, and they belonged to a wide variety of religious denominations. There were 88 American-Caucasians, 11 Austrian-Caucasians, 8 Chinese, 22 Filipinos, 32 Hawaiians, 20 Japanese, 21 Koreans, 11 other Asians (mostly Chinese), and 16 Samoans.

13. Sroufe, L. A. 1985. Attachment classification from the perspectives of infant-caregiver relationships and infant temperament. *Child Development.* 56:1-14.

14. Ball, J. A. 1987. *Reactions to Motherhood.* New York: Cambridge.

15. Beckman, L. 1978. The relative rewards and costs of parenthood and employment for employed women." *Psychology of Women Quarterly*, 2 (spring):3.

16. Yorrow, L. 1982. How to get your husband to help. Parents, 55 (May). 17

17. Selye, H. 1974. *Stress without Distress.* NewYork: L. B. Lippincott.

18. Eliot, R. 1983. Stress: can we cope? *Time* (June 6).

19. Hoffman, L. W. and Hoffman, M. L. 1973. The value of children to parents. In J. T. Fawcett (ed.), *Psychological Perspectives on Population.* New York: Basic Books, 19-76.

20. Psalms 127:3.

21. LaRossa, R. 1986. *Becoming a Parent.* Beverly Hills, CA: Sage.

22. Lamb, M. E. 1978. The father's role in the infant's social world. In J. H. Stevens and Matthew (eds.) *Mother/Child, Father/Child Relationships*, Washington, D.C.: National Association for the Education of Young Children.

23. Parke, R. D. and Tinsley, B. R. 1981. The father's role in infancy: determinants of involvement in caregiving and play. In M. E. Lamb (ed.) *The Role of the Father in Child Development* (2nd ed). New York: Wiley-Interscience 429-457. And Lamb, M. E. 1978. The father's role in the infant's social world. In J. H. Stevens, and Mathew (eds.). *Mother/Child, Father/Child Relationships*. Washington D.C.: National Association for the Education of Young Children.

24. Pleck. J. H. 1985. *Working Wives/Working Husbands*, Beverly Hills, CA: Sage.

25. Rexroat, C. and Shehan, C. 1987. The family life cycle and spouses' time in housework. *Journal of Marriage and the Family* 49:737-750.

26. Miller, J. B. 1987. *Psychology of Women*. Boston: Beacon Press.

27. Jensen and Kingston. 1988. *Parenting*. Olt, Rinehart and Winston, Inc. New York. And Jensen, J. and Petersen, G. 1987. *Merely Mothering and Other Myths*. Salt Lake City: Shadow Mountain.

28. Parke, R. D. and O'Leary. S. E. 1976. Father/mother/infant interaction in the newborn period: some findings, some observations and some unresolved issues. In K. F. Riegel and J. A. Meacham (eds.) *The Developing Individual in a Changing World: Social and Environmental Issues*. Chicago: Aldine.

29. Schaffer, H. R. and Emerson, P. E. 1964. The development of social attachments in infancy. *Monographs of the Society for Research in Child Development* 29 (3):1-150.

30. Yarrow, M. R. Scott, R., and Waxler, C. Z. 1973. Learning concern for others. *Developmental Psychology* 8:240-260.

31. Sears, R., Maccoby, E., and Levin, H. 1957. *Patterns of Childrearing*. Evanston, IL: Row Peterson.

32. McClelland, C. A., Constantian, R. D., and Stone, C. 1978. Making it to maturity. *Psychology Today* 12:42+.

33. Parke, R. D. and Sawin, D. B. 1977. Fathering: it's a major role. *Psychology Today* 12: 42+.

34. Baumrind, D. 1971.Current patterns of parental authority. *Developmental Psychology Monographs* 4:101.

35. Ibid. For further reading, Hurlock, E. B. 1989. *Development Psychology:* A Life-Span Approach. New York: McGraw-Hill, 133-34.

36. Thomas, A. S., Chess, and Birch, H. G. 1970. The origin of personality. *Scientific American* 223:109.

37. Carey, W. B. and McDevitt, S. C. 1978. Stability and change in individual temperament diagnosis from infancy to childhood. *Journal of the American Academy of Child Psychiatry* 17:331-337

38. Bradburn, N. M. and Caplovitz, D. 1965. *Reports on Happiness: A Pilot Study of Behavior Related to Mental Health.* Chicago: Aldine.

39. Hurlock, E. B. 1972. *Child Development.* New York: McGraw-Hill, 205-206.

40. Maccoby, E. 1980. *Social Development: Psychological Growth and the Parent-Child Relationship.* New York: Harcourt Brace Jovanovich, 382.

41. Ibid., 382-383..

42. Baumrind, D. 1967. Child care practices anteceding three patterns of preschool behavior. *Genetic Psychology Monographs* 75:43-88. And Staub, E. 1979. *Positive Social Behavior and Morality* (2nd ed.). New York: Academic, 189-194.

43. Macarou, D. 1970. *Incentives to Work.* San Francisco: Josey Bass, 62-70. 44

44. Zanden, V. W. 1981. *Human Development* (2nd ed.). New York: Knopf, 364.

45. Hebb. D. O. 1955. Drives and the CNS (conceptual nervous system). *Psychological Review* 62:234-254.

46. McCandless, B. R. 1967. *Children: Behavior and Development* (2nd ed.). New York: Holt, Rinehart, and Winston, 268, 282.

Ibid., 268.

Ibid., 282.

47. Tolstoy, L. 1882. *My Confession*. Quoted in W. James. 1920. *The Varieties of Religious Experiences*. New York: Longman's Green, 153-155.

48. Coleman, J. C. 1974. *Contemporary Psychology and Effective Behavior*. Glenville, Il: Scott Foreman and Co., 11.

49. Moustakas, C. E. 1977. *Creative Life*. New York: D. Van Norstrand. Ibid., 77.

50. Frankl, V. 1962. *Man's Search for Meaning*. New York: Simon and Schuster.

51. Maslow, A.H. 1943. A dynamic theory of human motivation. *Psychological Review* 50:375.

52. Ibid., 378.

53. Oswald. 1962. *Sleeping and Waking*. New York: Elsevier.

54. Scrimshaw, N. and Gordon, J. E. 1968. *Malnutrition, Learning, and Behavior*. Cambridge, MA: MIT Press.

55. Shineor, E. 1974. *The Malnourished Mind*. Garden City, NY: Anchor Press/Doubleday, 68-72.

56. Skinner, B. F. 1953. *Science and Human Behavior*. New York: Macmillan.

57. Walters, G. C. and Grusec, J. E. 1977. *Punishment*. San Francisco, CA: Freeman.

58. Norton, R .G. 1977. *Parenting*. Englewood Cliffs, NJ: Prentice-Hall.

59. Krumboltz, J. P. and Krumboltz, H. B. 1972. *Changing Children's Behavior*. Englewood Cliffs, NJ: Prentice-Hall.

60. Zimmerman, E. H. and Zimmerman, J. 1962. The alteration of behavior in a special classroom situation. *Journal Experimental Analysis of Behavior* 5:59-60.

61. Dreikurs, R. 1948. *The Challenge of Parenthood*. New York: Duell, Sloan, and Pearce.

62. Dreikurs, R. 1968. *Psychology in the Classroom*. New York: Duell, Sloan, and Pearce.

63. Dreikurs, R. and Grey, L. 1968. *Logical Consequences: A Handbook of Discipline*. New York: Meredith.

64. Dreikurs, R. and Soltz V. 1967. *Children the Challenge*. New York: Duell, Sloan and Pearce.

65. Gordon. T. 1970. Parent Effectiveness Training, N.Y. Wyder p. 130.

66. Gordon, T. 1970. Parent Effectiveness Training, N.Y. Wyder p. 234..

67. Hoffman, M. 1970. Moral development. In P. H. Mussen (ed.) *Carmichael's Manual of Child Development*. New York: Wiley.

68. Bandura, A. 1977. The role of modeling processes in personality development. In W. W.Hartup and N. L. Smothergill (eds.) *The Child: Reviews of Research*. Washington, D.C.: N.A.E.Y.C., 43. See also Bandura, A. and Walters, R.H. 1959. *Adolescent Aggression*. New York: Ronald Press.

68. Bandura, A. 1977. The role of modeling processes in personality development. In W. W.Hartup and N. L. Smothergill (eds.) The *Child: Reviews of Research*. Washington, D.C.: N.A.E.Y.C., 43.

69. Hoffman, J. L. 1976. Empathy, role-taking, guilt, and development of altruistic motives. In T. Lichons (ed.) *Moral Development and Behavior*. New York: Holt, Rinehart, and Winston.

70. Glasser, W. 1965. *Reality Therapy: A New Approach to Psychiatry*. New York: Harper and Row, 236-242.

71. Methvin, E. H. 1975. What you can do about TV violence. *Reader's Digest*, (July) 185.

72. Meyer, W. J. and Dusek, J. B. 1979. *Child Psychology: A Developmental Perspective*. Lexington, MA: D.C. Heath.

ABOUT PROFESSOR JENSEN

Professor Jensen was born in 1938 and grew up in Wyoming, Montana, and Colorado. He is married to Janet and is father to 10 children, 33 grandchildren, and 3 great grandchildren.

After graduating from Wheat Ridge High School in Colorado he received B.S. and M.S. Degrees from Brigham Young University and his Ph.D. degree from Michigan State University.

Professor Jensen has taught at the following universities:

1. Michigan State University
2. State University of New York at Potsdam
3. Brigham Young University at Provo
4. Brigham Young University at Hawaii
5. Utah State University

He has consulted for:

1. Research for Better Schools
2. Journal of Child Development
3. Psychological Reports and Perceptual Motor Skills
4. Family Research Center Brigham Young University
5. Provo and Salt Lake City Public Schools
6. Institute for Population Studies

His books include the following:

1. What's Right What's Wrong
2. Understanding and Using Social Influence Techniques
3. That's Not Fair
4. Moral Reasoning: A Philosophical and Psychological Intergration
5. Responsibility and Morality
6. Feelings: Helping Children Understand Emotions
7. History of Moral Education

8. Stepping Into Step-Parenting

9. Adolescence

10. Parenting: An Applied Textbook

11. Family Feminism

12. Families: The Key to a Prosperous and Compassionate Society in the 21ˢᵗ Century

He has published multiple scholarly articles in the following journals:

1. Psychological Reports

2. Utah Personnel and Guidance Association Research Bulletin

3. Proceedings of the American Educational Research Association

4. Journal of Educational Psychology

5. Developmental Psychology

6. Journal of Experimental Psychology

7. Journal of Genetic Psychology

8. British Journal of Social and Clinical Psychology

9. Journal of Moral Education

10. Education

11. Educational and Psychological Measurement

12. Psychology in the Schools

13. Sex Roles

14. Journal of Psychology

15. Adolescence

16. International Journal of Social Psychiatry

17. Youth and Society

18. Journal for the Scientific Study or Religion

19. Journal of Business Ethics

20. Family Perspectives

21. Journal of Personality Assessment

22. American Educational Research Journal

23. Addictive Behaviors

24. Journal of Cross Cultural Psychology

25. Journal of Research and Development in Education

26. Family Therapy

27. Religion and Public Education

28. The Family in America

29. Youth and Adolescence

www.ingramcontent.com/pod-product-compliance
Lightning Source LLC
Chambersburg PA
CBHW060903120626
46553CB00001B/192